Beyond the Archives

Beyond
the Archives
Research as a Lived Process

Edited by Gesa E. Kirsch and Liz Rohan
With a Foreword by Lucille M. Schultz

Southern Illinois University Press
Carbondale

11 10 09 08   4 3 2 1

Chapter 1 copyright © 2008 by David Gold. Chapter 10 copyright © 2008 by Gail Y. Okawa.
Chapter 11 copyright © 2008 by W. Ralph Eubanks. Chapter 12 copyright © 2008 by Malea
Powell. Chapter 16 copyright © 2008 by Anca Vlasopolos. An earlier version of chapter 2,
by Gesa E. Kirsch, was published in *Peitho: Newsletter of the Coalition of Women Scholars in
the History of Rhetoric and Composition*. The poem "It Is Raining Today," by Sandra María
Esteves, reprinted in chapter 9, is copyright © 1984 by Sandra María Esteves, from *Tropical
Rain: A Bilingual Downpour* by Sandra María Esteves (New York: African Caribbean Poetry
Theater, 1984; 30 pp). The poem by Muin Ozaki reprinted in chapter 10 is from *Poets behind
Barbed Wire*, ed. and trans. Jiro Nakano and Kay Nakano (Honolulu: Bamboo Ridge Press,
1983, 18); used with permission from Kay Kyoko Yokoyama. Quotations from Cynthia Carr
and from Deb Margolin in chapter 13 are used with permission.

Library of Congress Cataloging-in-Publication Data
Beyond the archives : research as a lived process / edited by Gesa E. Kirsch and Liz Rohan ;
with a foreword by Lucille M. Schultz.
    p. cm.
Includes bibliographical references.
ISBN-13: 978-0-8093-2840-6 (pbk. : alk. paper)
ISBN-10: 0-8093-2840-2 (pbk. : alk. paper)
   1. English language—Rhetoric—Research 2. History—Methodology. 3. History—Archival
resources. 4. Archives—Research—Case studies. I. Kirsch, Gesa. II. Rohan, Liz, 1967–
PE1404.B49 2008
001.4—dc22   2007027459

Printed on recycled paper. ♻

The paper used in this publication meets the minimum requirements of American National
Standard for Information Sciences—Permanence of Paper for Printed Library Materials,
ANSI Z39.48-1992. ∞

Contents

Foreword VII
   Lucille M. Schultz

Acknowledgments XI

Introduction: The Role of Serendipity, Family Connections,
and Cultural Memory in Historical Research   1
   Gesa E. Kirsch and Liz Rohan

PART ONE. WHEN SERENDIPITY, CREATIVITY, AND PLACE
COME INTO PLAY

1. The Accidental Archivist: Embracing Chance and
   Confusion in Historical Scholarship   13
      David Gold

2. Being on Location: Serendipity, Place, and
   Archival Research   20
      Gesa E. Kirsch

3. Getting to Know Them: Concerning Research into
   Four Early Women Writers   28
      Christine Mason Sutherland

4. Making Connections   37
      Alicia Nitecki

PART TWO. WHEN PERSONAL EXPERIENCE, FAMILY HISTORY,
AND RESEARCH SUBJECTS INTERSECT

5. Traces of the Familiar: Family Archives as Primary
   Source Material   47
      Wendy B. Sharer

6. The Biography of a Graveyard   56
      Ronald R. Stockton

7. In a Treeless Landscape: A Research Narrative   66
      Kathleen Wider

8. My Grandfather's Trunk   73
   Barry Rohan

**PART THREE. WHEN PERSONAL, CULTURAL, AND HISTORICAL
MEMORY SHAPE THE POLITICS OF THE ARCHIVES**

9. Colonial Memory, Colonial Research: A Preamble to a
   Case Study   83
   Victor Villanueva

10. Unbundling: Archival Research and Japanese American
    Communal Memory of U.S. Justice Department
    Internment, 1941–45   93
    Gail Y. Okawa

11. Mississippi on My Mind   107
    W. Ralph Eubanks

12. Dreaming Charles Eastman: Cultural Memory,
    Autobiography, and Geography in Indigenous
    Rhetorical Histories   115
    Malea Powell

13. Cultural Memory and the Lesbian Archive   128
    Kate Davy

**PART FOUR. WHEN THE LIVES OF OUR RESEARCH SUBJECTS
PARALLEL OUR OWN**

14. "I See Dead People": Archive, Crypt, and an Argument
    for the Researcher's Sixth Sense   139
    Elizabeth (Betsy) Birmingham

15. Stitching and Writing a Life   147
    Liz Rohan

16. When Two Stories Collide, They Catch Fire   154
    Anca Vlasopolos

17. Stumbling in the Archives: A Tale of Two Novices   161
    Lisa Mastrangelo and Barbara L'Eplattenier

Contributors   171

Foreword

Lucille M. Schultz

Beyond the Archives: Research as a Lived Process marks the change from reading an archive not just as a source but also as a subject. That is, the authors of these interdisciplinary research narratives understand archives, in the words of anthropologist Ann Laura Stoler, not as "things" but as "epistemological experiments"; not as sites of "knowledge retrieval" but as sites of "knowledge production" (87, 90). And thus the essays in this collection instantiate the archival turn that scholars have theorized in recent years. With graceful accounts, the authors invite readers to accompany them on their research journeys, revealing for us the ways in which the paths they travel are marked by twists and turns, with forward steps and backward steps, with detours and side trips—all this as part of their research as a lived process, all this as part of the collection's significant intellectual work.

Individually and as a collection, the essays here demonstrate the difference between "history as event" and "history as account." When an event has taken place, what we know of it comes from various accounts constructed as rhetorical acts in a theoretical space by writers who, while engaged in historical research, assume the subject positions of rhetorician. No longer, for example, do we argue about whether writers are affected by what Kenneth Burke called terministic screens; we know we are. A particularly strong feature of these first-person narratives is that the writers name the subjectivities with which they intentionally and unavoidably approach the print materials, the ephemera, and the physical sites they interrogate. Writers also shed light on the institutional interests and the subjectivities that are served by an established archive, and not only by records in the archive but even by buildings that house the records. Working with the letters of Native American elder Charles Eastman at the Newberry Library in Chicago, Malea Powell recalls in her essay that the Newberry and its records of imperialism were built and collected on land where the Miami tribes once harvested garlic. In Gesa E. Kirsch's essay, a project that explores the life, work, and rhetorical agency of Dr. Mary Bennett Ritter, Kirsch reminds us that whether reading or constructing an archive, a researcher is also interpreting: archival records are never simply transparent. Just as a collection of records is established from an interested perspective, it is also read from an interested perspective.

Also in this collection, the writers demonstrate the complexities of constructing an archive for a particular audience and purpose, recognizing that just as the histories we construct are contingent and limited, so, too, are the repositories in which we work. As our kitchen counters, refrigerator doors, desks, filing cabinets, photo albums, junk drawers, and electronic files remind us, we interact with records, many and varied, on a daily basis. And we routinely make decisions—sometimes deliberately, sometimes randomly—about which records to keep and which to toss; we see the results of these decisions in every family's personal papers. Barbara Slater Smith, my husband David Smith's mother, was an elementary teacher in a public school in Columbus, Ohio; I was not lucky enough to know her, but in one of the schoolbooks she used, a book called *Fundamentals of German*, is tucked a yellowed, handwritten note: a March 1937 report of a supervisor who had observed her sixth grade class. Did Barbara Smith keep that note because of its praise and encouragement? And what of the other reports that she didn't keep? Here, in Barry Rohan's essay "My Grandfather's Trunk," we learn of the miscellaneous, unsystematically saved documents that Rohan found in that trunk, documents that led him to other documents and thus allowed him to write the story of a career.

So, too, professional archivists make decisions about those records that will be available to future generations as part of a collective cultural memory. Their criteria include not only those specific to an institution's mission but also those that might affect an institution's holdings at a given moment; something as simple as "available space," for example, could be a factor in decision-making. And an archivist is always committed to the key principles that govern the establishment of an archival collection: provenance (*respect des fonds*), which entails avoiding any intermingling of records from various collections, and the sanctity of the original order (*respect pour l'ordre primitif*), which requires faithfulness to the creator's sequence. The effect of these many processing decisions, both big and small, is that for a particular project, a writer is not likely to find all of the records he or she needs in a single collection, in a single location. It's in this circumstance, working outside of an established, searchable collection, that we compose what rhetoric scholar Shirley Rose calls a "physically dispersed but intellectually integrated archive." Alicia Nitecki, in her essay "Making Connections," offers a stunning example of how her purposeful and accidental finds of books, letters, essays, phone books, and personal contacts allowed her to uncover a long-suppressed Polish work on the Holocaust. Victor Villanueva pulls together family stories, biography, FBI reports, photos, and a gag order to understand how Dr. Pedro Albizu Campos, a graduate of Harvard Law School, a veteran of the U.S. military, and a Christian Democrat "who believed that Puerto Rico and its people should be free," spent most of his life in prison because he wrote twelve speeches—speeches that never sparked a revolution but were considered "dangerously revolutionary."

The authors here model for us the ways in which cultural theorists extend the definition of archive beyond print records or ephemera. Kate Davy finds that the cultural memory that she sought was archived in performances of Women's One World theater and festivals. Ronald R. Stockton works with the inscriptions on grave markers in a cemetery that dates back to 1840, exploring how monuments as well as landscape history can be read as part of an archive. And Liz Rohan points to the ways that Avery Street in Detroit, a street where writer Janette Miller lived, became for Rohan an historic, architectural, and geographic "text."

Finally to say, the authors of these narratives articulate their methodologies, both planned and unplanned, and the emotions that accompany their work. As a scholar who has worked for almost two decades in more than a dozen archives, ranging from the Library of Congress and Harvard's many libraries to the New Harmony Workingmen's Institute in New Harmony, Indiana, and the archive of the American School for the Deaf in Hartford, Connecticut, I found myself, as I read, identifying more than once with a writer's disappointment at not finding a much sought-after record, with a writer's joy at an unexpected find, with a writer's nagging sense that there must be something else out there, and, perhaps above all, with the passion for research that is embedded in each of these accounts. Archival research can be a lonely enterprise. By naming the ways in which their work touches their lives, and the ways in which their lives touch their work, the writers of these narratives help those of us who do historical research become part of a collective enterprise, encouraged by knowing that when the research trail takes an unexpected turn or meets a dead end, or even veers off the road into a ditch, we are in good company.

The major contribution of this work, in sum, is not just that the writers construct new histories, though they do that persuasively. More powerfully, these authors present their work to readers not as a fait accompli but rather as a lived process. In no other cultural memory work that I know of do the writers articulate their methodologies with as much inflection and nuance—and thus with self-awareness and reflection—as the writers do here. Not only, therefore, do these writers make an archival turn with their work, they also make a writerly turn in the ways they present it to us—and readers are the richer for that. Accomplished editors and scholars Gesa E. Kirsch and Liz Rohan bring forward a collection of narratives grounded in records of human needs and activities, a collection that becomes its own double as it earns a well-deserved place as a first-rate record of groundbreaking scholarship. *Viva.*

Works Cited

Rose, Shirley. E-mail to the author. February 19, 2007.
Stoler, Ann Laura. "Colonial Archives and the Art of Governance." *Archival Science* 2 (2002): 87–109.

Acknowledgments

Together, Gesa E. Kirsch and Liz Rohan would like to thank the contributors for sharing their stories of discovery, serendipity, and inspiration; for their care and thoughtfulness revising their work; and for their graciousness and patience with the editing and publishing process. We are also indebted to Catherine Hobbs and Lucille M. Schultz for their helpful feedback and suggestions and to Karl Kageff, editor-in-chief at Southern Illinois University Press, for his support, enthusiasm, and leadership.

Gesa Kirsch would like to thank the archivists who have inspired her work, supported her many requests, and led her to unexpected discoveries. In particular, I would like to thank Deborah Day at the Scripps Institution of Oceanography, University of California, San Diego; Patty French at the Lane Medical Library, Stanford University; and David Kessler at the Bancroft Library, University of California, Berkeley.

I am grateful to Bentley College for summer support and travel grants to conduct archival research. Many thanks go to my colleagues in the English department, especially George Ellenbogen, Maureen Goldman, and Barbara Paul-Emile, who followed my archival adventures with interest, support, and enthusiasm.

Friends and family members were close during the years of working on this book. Warm thanks to Ann Bonner for making time to visit often; to Marlowe Miller and David Keevil for years of friendship; and to Pauline Donnelly and Joe Selvaggi for sharing training runs and martinis and for helping us find our new home.

I am grateful to members of my family who traveled far and visited often during the last few years: Werner Kirsch and Christa Möllers; Gunder Brotchie; Karl Kirsch and Mall Koiv; Thomas Müller; and Dorothea Herreiner. A special thanks goes to my dad, Hans Otto Kirsch, for his support and encouragement from afar.

Two new and unexpected friends deserve special mention. Jim Fraser—serendipity once again—has been most wonderful in getting me on the road to a new adventure, and Steven M. Greenberg at Vilna Shul: The Boston Center for Jewish Heritage has been a great neighbor and enthusiastic supporter of my work.

Acknowledgments

With deep gratitude, I express thanks to those who came before me and still make their presence felt in my life—Elisabeth Wernich Kirsch, always close in spirit; Ingeborg Thoeming Kirsch, whom I have gotten to know only lately through family stories; Katharina Kirsch, dearly missed and beloved; and Dr. Mary Bennett Ritter, whom I have met only vicariously, on the page and in the archives, but who remains a great source of inspiration.

Finally, and most especially, I would like to thank Tony Schreiner for many years of friendship, love, and laughter.

Liz Rohan would like to thank the staff at the Bentley Historical Library at the University of Michigan for their wonderful resources, including the Bordin/Gillette Researcher Travel fellowship. Thanks also to Joan Duffy at the Yale Divinity Library, who was a continual source of information during my research trip to the library and thereafter, when I had questions regarding citations.

The University of Michigan–Dearborn supported conference trips that led to my conversations with Gesa about this project. My mentors at the University of Illinois—Gail Hawisher, Peter Mortensen, Paul Prior, and Bill Kelleher—also helped me when a graduate student and now in spirit, as also do my fellow graduate students: Joyce Walker, Karen Lunsford, Mary Sheridan-Rabideau, Renee Thomas Pyrtel, and Amanda Shepard.

Thanks to other friends who supported my scholarly endeavors and have read my works in progress: Liz Gonzalez, Beth Burmester, Cindy Rawson, and David Gold. Thanks especially to my friend/cousin Cathy Kenny, who always knows I can do it.

Janette Miller, although deceased, somehow still helped me get home—a place I wouldn't know I needed to be otherwise, which I'm grateful for every day.

Finally, and especially, I thank my parents, Kathy and Barry, and my brother, Brendan, for their spiritual and material support over the long haul.

Beyond the Archives

Introduction

The Role of Serendipity, Family Connections, and Cultural Memory in Historical Research

Gesa E. Kirsch and Liz Rohan

In her memoir *French Lessons*, Duke professor Alice Kaplan writes that literary critic and Yale professor Paul de Man "would have been a better teacher if he had given more of his game away" because she believes "the root of [his] intellectual questions was his own experience and pain" (172, 173). A former student of his at Yale, Kaplan points out that de Man's interest in nationalism and his prized method of text interpretation, deconstruction, can be traced to his experience living in German-occupied Belgium and his authorship of fascist, pro-Nazi texts. Although Kaplan had been writing her dissertation about fascism when a student with him, de Man maintained the illusion that his scholarly projects were disinterested, not, as she would discover upon his death, arguably linked to his intriguing, checkered, and likely tortured past. In *French Lessons*, Kaplan gives *her* game away by describing how the memory of her lawyer father, a prosecutor at the Nuremberg trials who died when Kaplan was eight, led Kaplan to French, France itself, and eventually to academe, where she is a successful scholar. Kaplan's experience suggests, then, that how a researcher chooses a subject is a subject unto itself.

The occasion for putting together this collection has illustrated for us the many more stories like Kaplan's and the value of researchers "giving their game away." Once we invited contributions on the process of finding and sustaining a research project, we learned about the connections woven through so many of our scholarly and personal lives that remain largely unarticulated. The essays in this collection demonstrate how virtual, historical, and lived experiences intersect, particularly as researchers extract meaning from sources in locations most associated with isolation and loneliness—the archives. They show that research does not just take place in the library archives but also when researchers pursue supplementary information and additional perspectives about their data from existing people and places. The focus of many of the essays in the book is on archival and historical research, but all tell tales of fascinating discoveries, unexpected leads, and early hunches leading to a scholarly project.

Beyond the Archives illustrates the range of research methods and strategies available to scholars, such as using space and location as a way to understand the sites where a historical subject lived; using oral histories and interviews with local informants or relatives to better understand the actors involved in shaping the politics, culture, and history of the times; and being attentive to unexpected leads or chance encounters that can enrich a research project as well as change its direction and scope. Second, this collection enriches our notion of what constitutes an archive. Contributors use materials from regional and local sources, family records and artifacts, even FBI and other government documents. By doing so, they highlight how using these less frequently consulted resources can enrich our understanding of history, culture, and rhetoric. Finally, we see this book contributing to a sense of excitement, discovery, and inspiration in doing research, a facet of research that we consider crucial to sustaining the long-term interest and passion of scholars. This, in turn, is necessary to produce the most thorough, complete, and engaged scholarly work. The collection on the whole addresses what inspires our work, what attracts us to our research subjects, how they attract us, and the role of serendipity, place, and cultural memory in making knowledge.

Most contributors are scholars in the field of composition and rhetoric, but others work in fields like philosophy, Holocaust studies, creative writing, theater studies, political science, and freelance journalism. Overall, writers in this volume unpack their thinking in process and help readers see how they have mined their lives for meaningful patterns when shaping analysis and casting impressions of their research subjects. Thus, these writers indeed teach, as Kaplan suggests, by making the research process more transparent by describing it. Most important, they show why anyone would embark on research in the first place. For these writers, research is a meaningful collection process that has helped them better understand their own historically situated experience. It can even become an identity-forming, life-changing activity. Therefore, this book can be a guide for composition and rhetoric students who are beginning archival work and may also bring depth and comprehension for seasoned scholars in the field who are not historians by training but use archives for their work. The essays can also be useful for teachers across the humanities because these short, jargon-free pieces make comprehensible the interpretive skills that researchers bring to their projects.

Expanded Notions of the Archive: Including Family, Local, and Genealogical History

Linda Ferreira-Buckley points out that in the late twentieth century, attitudes shifted about what "counts" as archival material worthy of academic study. She argues that research methods should parallel these developments. The research described in this volume shows the results of an expanded conception of archives. Many of these researchers have used regional and familial archives for their data collection and analysis. Their work teaches the value of attending to how our family, social, and cultural history is intertwined with more traditional notions of history and culture. It helps us understand and explore the fissures of historical narratives, the places at the margins where voices have been suppressed, silenced, or ignored. Furthermore, these essays show that researching family archives and local stories can and does lead to sustained scholarly work and contributes to new knowledge, both in and outside of academe.

For instance, W. Ralph Eubanks discovered that his parents were placed on a secret watch list by the state of Mississippi. That this placement constituted a significant threat to his family's safety, well-being, and survival led Eubanks to engage in serious, scholarly research and the publication of his book, *Ever Is a Long Time: A Journey into Mississippi's Dark Past*. This topic, which came to light only with the release of the Sovereignty Commission files in the late 1990s, adds a personal dimension to Eubanks's research and, we argue, highlights the historical impact, seriousness, and threat that was experienced by Eubanks's family and hundreds of others like it. Eubanks's research also suggests that family history cannot be extricated from public history because individual lives shape and are shaped by the times—as in the segregated American South of Eubanks's childhood. As a consequence, writers who discuss family members in our collection create and report interpretations not just about their families and themselves but about the larger world as well.

The intersection of the personal, cultural, and scholarly aspects of our lives emerged as an important new site for original scholarship among our contributors. Personal archives, relatives' scrapbooks, and papers discovered under a grandmother's bed or in the attic led these researchers to see their own relatives as actors shaping and shaped by a larger history, History with a capital *H*, while they learn more about their own histories. For contributor Wendy B. Sharer, for example, one small box of family memories she found in her grandmother's closet led her to write a book about post-suffrage clubs and, in the meantime, helped Sharer better appreciate her grandmother's life as a member of such clubs. A similar discovery, a trunk found in the basement of his mother's apartment building, led Barry Rohan to the papers of his grandfather, a Hollywood scriptwriter, whom he had been named after but never met. For Victor Villanueva, his father's death inspired, in part, his curiosity about his Puerto Rican heritage and the speeches of Puerto Rican revolutionary Pedro Albizu Campos, who had once dated his father's sister. Similarly, the death of Ronald R. Stockton's father precipitated an interest in the local cemetery of his southern Illinois hometown, which led to a scholarly article about this cemetery. For each of these researchers, like several others in this collection, families supplied key sources or became sources themselves for research.

Curiosity and Serendipity: Moving from a Chance Encounter to Scholarly Research

In addition to expanding a narrow conception of archives, the experiences narrated in this volume teach the importance of attending to facets of the research process that might easily be marginalized and rarely mentioned because they seem merely intuitive, coincidental, or serendipitous. These authors illustrate the mostly undocumented phenomenon that a commitment to a research subject might begin with a simple clue. Authors show how they moved from a hunch, a chance encounter, or a newly discovered family artifact to scholarly research. For instance, contributor David Gold's current research on the history of rhetorical education at non-elite American colleges, which led to his forthcoming book, *Rhetoric at the Margins: Revising the History of Writing Instruction in American Colleges, 1873–1947*, grew from a happy accident. He was reading an article in the local paper about a ceremony honoring a graduate of historically black Huston-Tillotson College in Austin, Texas. This clue led him to a trail of archival material about non-elite college composition programs, his doctoral dissertation topic, and his book project.

If Gold's curiosity had not been sparked by reading that article, or if he had considered this story "merely" a local one and therefore uninteresting or unimportant to the academic community, he would not have conducted his extensive research on rhetorical education in non-elite colleges, a topic that has made an important contribution to our understanding of the history of rhetoric and writing studies. Experiences like Gold's instruct us that unless we pay serious attention to aspects of our lived experience that connect us with insight, intuition, and creativity, we might lose out on many leads that can enrich our understanding of past and present, virtual and historical experiences. And if new researchers censor this very real and useful aspect of the research process, they might not learn to trust or recognize their own hunches.

That is not to say that serendipity is necessary for identifying a good research topic; in fact, coincidence, chance, or luck may not come into play at all. We consider genuine curiosity, a willingness to follow all possible leads, an openness to what one may encounter, and flexibility in revising research questions and the scope of a project to be key factors for conducting successful historical work. Gold's research illustrates this process: he pursued an interest sparked by reading the local newspaper and then began the hard work of sustained research—visiting archives, refocusing and expanding the topic as he learned more, reading in the field to see what kinds of histories of writing instruction already existed, and figuring out how the new information he was gathering could enrich our understanding of rhetorical education.

Serendipity and genuine curiosity nevertheless also had a part in Gesa E. Kirsch's research about the life and writings of Dr. Mary Bennett Ritter, a nineteenth-century physician, women's rights advocate, and civic leader. Kirsch's visit to Ritter's stomping grounds in Berkeley, California, included a stay at a hotel that had once housed the women's club where Ritter had done work with a women's honor society. Kirsch's discovery of Ritter's portrait in the hotel's sitting room, along with a study of Ritter's papers "on location," deepened Kirsch's intellectual attachment to Ritter.

Engaging with family resources as well as studying "place" have been methods Kathleen Wider found useful when writing her book *In a Treeless Landscape*, which describes her grandmother's unusual role as a speaker on the national lecture circuit on such topics as art, beauty, and the development of individuals and citizens. Wider's research shows that nontraditional research methods—such as looking up old court records, walking the section line of her grandmother's family homestead in South Dakota, and interviewing people who knew her grandmother or her family or who knew the land—gave her a depth of understanding of her grandmother's life that she could not have gotten if she had relied solely on traditional academic research methods.

Thus, *place* as archive is another major lesson of research promoted by these contributors and their research experiences. When Christine Mason Sutherland, for example, writes about going to locations in England—Lancashire, London, and Norwich—to research the lives and writing of four early women writers, she argues that exploring the places of deceased or historical subjects helps researchers avoid "presentism" in historical research. Kirsch's, Sutherland's, and Wider's research exemplifies how visiting the geographical location where a historical subject lived and worked is another important, if undertheorized, research method. Exploring a place and re-seeing a place as an archive teach the hands-on nature of research. This method of research is intricately linked with living, being present both mindfully and physically.

Cultural Memory and Identity: Speaking Back to the Archives

Gail Y. Okawa, like Kirsch, Wider, and Sutherland, used living places—New Mexico and Hawaii—as archives for making meaning when researching the conditions of her Japanese American grandfather's internment during World War II. Okawa's research, like several of the stories collected here, also teaches that not all research experiences are "happy" ones. Archives can re-inscribe power structures and imperialist discourse, particularly when the researcher is both the object and the subject of research. For instance, when Malea Powell, a Native American scholar, visited the archives—the St. Louis Law Library's Native American Reference Collection—she found herself and her heritage the object of imperialist, colonial discourse. She had to work hard to maintain her sense of dignity in light of the demeaning discourse and records of injustices she encountered in the archives. This was also true for Victor Villanueva, whose research, mentioned previously, about Puerto Rican revolutionary Albizu Campos resulted in recovering forgotten contexts for both personal and cultural memories. In each case, these researchers had to find ways to "speak back" to the archives, to resist the imperialist discourse they encountered, and to connect to communities and cultural memory that reside outside of the traditional archives.

Okawa's, Powell's, and Villanueva's work teaches furthermore that research can resurrect the memory of historical actors to the extent that researchers bring previously repressed or hidden pasts to life. Hence, historical lives can shape the present as researchers work with and publish their data. When, for example, Kate Davy researched the performance rituals of 1970s New York City lesbian theater groups, she also recovered parts of the groups' cultural memory as the context of the erotically charged performances became lost with a new generation. In this case, the *process* of research itself creates new knowledge, not just published results. That is, researchers change and change others when they engage and make meaning of data, as they encounter people and places, and as they interpret and make meaning from archival data over the long course of a research project.

Virtual, Historical, and Lived Experiences: Connecting the Past and Present

Jacqueline Jones Royster theorizes that research subjects might serve as "teachers, mentors, [and] guides" aiding in a researcher's unrealized quest for "transformations" when confronting contemporary issues (278). In this sense, the resurrection of historical actors via research who are not family members can be as meaningful and transformative as learning more about family history. Several essays in this volume make visible this phenomenon of research theorized by Royster. Elizabeth (Betsy) Birmingham, for example, was one of the first scholars to write about female architect Marion Mahony Griffin, a contemporary of Frank Lloyd Wright, whose contributions to architectural design and architectural history had been repressed. Although Griffin died shortly before Birmingham was born, Birmingham feels she has a relationship with her and that she owes it to Griffin to tell her story. When authors like Birmingham disclose their engagement with their subjects whom they often "meet" only on paper, they admit the joyful human connections they have with their data, a phenomenon of research rarely articulated or made public.

Historical actors and contexts act on the culture now—and again—as researchers themselves grow and change over time when learning about their subjects and in turn act in their contemporary worlds. Birmingham, for example, was discouraged from writing about Griffin several years ago because Griffin was not interesting to Birmingham's male mentors. This contemporary experience with sexist attitudes eventually helped Birmingham to better imagine the sexism affecting Griffin's historical experience as a woman working in a male profession decades earlier. Likewise, Lisa Mastrangelo and Barbara L'Eplattenier's research on Progressive Era female writing program administrators seemed to both parallel and inform their contemporary collaborative work about these historical actors. Hence, the process of discovering and writing about research subjects helps researchers better imagine the struggles and experiences of these research subjects who were—like all of us—shaped by and constrained by their respective cultures.

Birmingham's experience further illustrates that researchers—particularly those working with marginalized archives or topics—may have to wait years for an audience to develop for their research. Birmingham's work on Griffin began nearly a decade ago, when she was an undergraduate student, but only now is there an emerging interest among architectural historians about Griffin in particular or women architects in general. Liz Rohan, similarly, found her research subject, missionary to Africa Janette Miller, when she was an undergraduate student over fifteen years ago. Rohan returned to this work over time in order to write about it and understand it. Only recently have feminists become interested in the historical women's missionary movement in America, allowing Rohan an audience for her data. Birmingham's and Rohan's stories, like all of the essays in this volume, further teach the value of research as a lived process. Doing research helps us understand our subjects, of course, but it guides us to see—for better or worse—how the world works.

Birmingham's and Rohan's experiences also point to the challenging, demanding, and at times slow nature of archival work. All researchers, and most especially novice researchers, need to set clear parameters in order to limit the scope of their projects. They need to be mindful of deadlines for degrees, publications, and tenure; further, they need to be realistic about travel expenses and the time, effort, and energy it takes to pursue archival research. In this book, we do *not* offer explicit guidelines about best archival research practices. For that kind of information, we suggest that readers consult *Peitho: Newsletter of the Coalition of Women Scholars in the History of Rhetoric and Composition* (which publishes occasional commentaries about practical aspects of archival research) and an edited collection in the works that promises to focus on the pragmatic aspects of archival work (L'Eplattenier, Mastrangelo, Sharer, and Ramsey).

That being said, we want to reiterate that archival research can be exciting, inspiring, even life-changing. We are convinced—and our chapters bear this out—that the most serious, committed, excellent historical research comes from choosing a subject to which we are personally drawn, whether through family artifacts, a chance encounter, a local news story, or some other fascination that sets us on a trail of discovery, curiosity, and intrigue. That personal connection can make all the difference in our scholarly pursuit: it brings the subject to life and makes us more likely to pursue hunches, follow leads, and spend extra time combing through archival materials than we would without a "personal attachment."

Untold Stories, Untapped Resources: Giving Our Game Away

Collectively, these essays promote themes of serendipity, chance discoveries, and personal connections as key ingredients for sustained research when working with archival documents. Much of the research described in this volume was inspired by a familial connection. Place, too, has been an important archive for almost all of these researchers. But we have organized the chapters to draw attention to important subthemes among the essays.

Essays in part 1 of the book feature the role of serendipity, creativity, and location as researchers like Gold and Kirsch discuss the clues outside of the archives they have pursued to make meaning of archives, including physical journeys, and literary scholar Alicia Nitecki traces the many connections she was able to make among living and deceased editors, writers, and graphic artists as she uncovered and translated the history of Polish Holocaust literature. Essays in part 2 highlight how the intersection of personal, cultural, and historical memory shapes research projects, particularly when a research subject is a relative, as it was for researchers like Wider, Sharer, and Barry Rohan. Essays in part 3 confront the politics of the archives, the charged experience when a researcher is both the object and subject of research, like it has been for writers Eubanks, Powell, and Okawa. Like many of the researchers in part 2, the subjects for some of these writers are relatives, or their experience was inspired by family memories or family archives. Essays in the final section of the book highlight the phenomenon whereby research subjects become guides and mentors as researchers' lived experiences seemingly parallel those of their deceased subjects—or when their research leads them to living people with whom they form a real relationship. This was the case for Anca Vlasopolos, who made a lifelong friend in Japan when pursuing the research for her historical novel.

As a collection, *Beyond the Archives* illustrates the importance of tapping into our passions, pursuing research subjects that attract our attention, and allowing creativity and intuition to enter the scholarly research process while broadening what "counts" as an archive. These essays outline where to start with a research project, how to keep going with a research project, and, most important, why research might be rewarding beyond the obvious rewards of getting a grant, getting a grade, or getting to know Grandpa. We hope this volume fosters the openness of heart and mind required for the very best scholarly work. We envision that readers will come away with glimpses into the individualized, fascinating windows each writer has shared in the chapters that follow. Each of these narratives shows that the best scholarly research is vital, exciting, done for its own sake, and—most often—results in more meaningful and reflective lives.

Works Cited

Ferreira-Buckley, Linda. "Rescuing the Archives from Foucault." *College English* 61.5 (1999): 577–83.

"Interview with Alice Kaplan, Author of *The Collaborator*, An: The Trial and Execution of Robert Brasillach." *University of Chicago Press*. 2000. <http://www.press.uchicago.edu/Misc/Chicago/424146in.html>.

Kaplan, Alice. *French Lessons: A Memoir*. Chicago: U of Chicago P, 1993.

Royster, Jacqueline Jones. *Traces of a Stream: Literacy and Social Change among African American Women*. Pittsburgh: U of Pittsburgh P, 2000.

Part One

When Serendipity, Creativity, and Place Come into Play

1

The Accidental Archivist
Embracing Chance and Confusion in Historical Scholarship

David Gold

I have a confession to make: I didn't plan on being a historian of rhetoric when I grew up. Instead, my research career began, like many of my colleagues', I suspect, with a happy accident—or rather a series of them.

I was not one of those frighteningly precocious graduate students who arrive on campus with their dissertation seemingly written but for the footnotes. I had little sense of English, my chosen field, as a discipline or of academia as a profession. Not surprisingly, my first year of graduate school did not go well. Though I was successful in my courses, I was having trouble connecting them to a scholarly path or even to my life outside of school. I had always loved the liberal arts and held a strong belief in education for its own sake. At the same time, I came from a working-class background that valued the practical, and a graduate degree in English, on the face of it, does not seem very practical. I had no idea how to mix these competing drives.

And then came my first happy accident: I discovered rhetoric. When I decided to attend the University of Texas at Austin, I did not realize that it was home to one of the strongest rhetoric and composition programs in the country. I didn't even know rhetoric was a discipline that could be studied. But after taking a course on the relationship among readers, writers, and texts, I was hooked. Rhetoric appealed both to my interest in education for its own sake and to my practical desire to be immersed in the world of experience beyond the academy. One of the oldest liberal arts, rhetoric has pragmatic roots—it originated as a means to help lay citizens participate in public discourse.

Now committed to the study of rhetoric, if still unsure what to do with it, I took a frustrating course in eighteenth- and nineteenth-century rhetoric. The course was frustrating for two reasons. First, this time period was an arguably bleak one for my field. Once the center of the liberal arts curriculum, rhetoric, by the late nineteenth century, had been reduced in the American academy to a single freshman course in composition, and not a very inspiring one at that.

Second, I was frustrated with the narrow focus of the historiography I was reading. Nearly every available text seemed to focus on events at the same few Ivy League institutions. I wasn't attending—or teaching in—an Ivy League institution, and yet we had an innovative rhetoric program. Surely other schools existed in the past where the rhetoric and composition curriculum was not so stifling, where students did not receive papers dripping with red ink, graded not for content but for form? And even if that were not the case, perhaps some first-generation college student at a state university might have welcomed the chance to study the finer points of prescriptive grammar if it meant an opportunity for socio-economic advancement? Not only did these histories narrowly represent the wide range of institutional experiences of American students, but they presumed that curricular innovation begins in elite colleges and thereafter filters down to less prestigious institutions.

Clearly, this is not always the case. Rensselaer, for example, was training engineers at a time when Harvard barely recognized science as a fit subject for a university. Teacher training in America began over sixty years before the establishment of Columbia's Teachers College. And Scottish public universities had as much or more influence on the shape of contemporary English studies in the American academy as did Oxford and Cambridge (Crawford; Horner; Miller). Unfortunately, at the time, I had no way to test my suspicions about the rhetorical tradition in American colleges; little research existed that even addressed, much less answered, my questions.

Then came the next happy accident.

One morning in the coffee shop, I picked up a copy of the local newspaper, which I infrequently read. In the local section was an article on a ceremony honoring Ilah Wright, 106 years old, a 1915 graduate of the city's historically black Huston-Tillotson College. Her daughter, Etta Robinson, in her seventies herself, recalled how her mother, upon her return to her home of Tyler, a small rural town in east Texas, acted as an informal community literacy liaison, reading and writing letters, checking contracts, and filling out government documents for neighbors: "Anything anybody had to do, any papers that needed to be filled out, they would come to my mother. . . . She was very happy that she went to school there" (qtd. in Thatcher).

I was awed by Ilah Wright and embarrassed by my ignorance. Here was an institution in my own community—just a ten-minute drive away—with a history as long and rich as that of my own university, and I knew almost nothing about it. How could I complain about the myopia of other scholars when I was guilty of the same thing myself? I decided to hit the archives.

Unfortunately, my first visit to Huston-Tillotson did not go well. Used to the free access and casual atmosphere of a large public institution, I was unprepared to do research in a small private one. When I called the library, I was told that the school had no archives and that old course catalogues, if they existed, would be housed in the registrar's office. Moreover, I would have to get permission from the registrar, the librarian told me doubtfully. So I called the registrar, who, after a pointed interrogation, allowed me to visit. Under her watchful eye, I made photocopies of crumbling catalogues on the office's old and noisy copy machine, surreptitiously scooping the book dust into my pocket lest she decide the material too fragile for me to work with. Every time I asked for another catalogue, I expected her to throw me out, but she merely frowned, took the old one out of my hand, and went into a back room to exchange it.

I felt clueless, a feeling I have since come to learn is at the heart of the scholarly process. In academia, one is in a perpetual liminal space. As soon as you answer a research question, you ask another, your growing body of expertise simply marking the expanding edge of your ignorance. Archival research especially exacerbates this condition. It's like putting together a jigsaw puzzle, except that you don't have a picture on the box for reference, there's more than one puzzle in the box, the picture keeps changing depending on how you fit the pieces together, and the pieces themselves change shape when your back is turned. Only slowly do the pieces begin to form a pattern. A 1927 report by a white observer lamenting the large number of African American high school students taking Latin and Greek instead of more "appropriate" vocational subjects illuminates the self-determination and courage in those educational choices; a few more such public critiques by other scholars and educational officials, and that choice of a classical curriculum begins to read more and more as an overt political act. The diary of the rural student at a women's college in the early 1920s recounting in detail the sweets the school served gives a human face to the simple demographic fact that most of the students came from families of modest means. The turn-of-the-twentieth-century normal school president who boxed his unruly students about the ears appears at first glance extreme and excessive until a contemporary master's thesis on education in the county recounts the ubiquity of corporal punishment without comment, and other archival sources suggest that professors in the region routinely packed pistols, such was the casual violence of the times.

Linda Ferreira-Buckley calls the process immersion, by which she means researchers must loose—and lose—themselves in the era they are studying. Not merely direct archival material but newspapers, textbooks, magazines, journals, encyclopedias, and other contemporary sources are essential because they provide historical context for the materials we work with.

So I immersed myself.

I was amazed to discover that Texas had eleven private black colleges before 1915 teaching a predominantly liberal arts curriculum. Moreover, these schools challenged what I had learned about the history of rhetoric. At a time when classical languages and oratory were moving to the periphery in Ivy League institutions, black colleges and high schools commonly offered four years of Latin and Greek and made oratory a central part of the curriculum. At a time when the flagship University of Texas was promoting current traditional rhetoric in its composition courses, Samuel Huston, Wiley, and other black colleges in Texas were using what was arguably the most progressive rhetoric textbook of the day. And not only did black colleges differ markedly from white institutions, but there was an enormous range of pedagogical diversity among black schools. There was a story here to be told.

When one of our department's senior scholars heard of my project, however, he pointedly let my advisor know that it would be "career suicide" for me to embark on it. This was also a fortunate event, though it did not seem so at the time. At first, I was angry. I felt like I was being asked to compromise my research for the sake of market realities. But I understood his point. At a composition conference one year, one of my colleagues, knowing of my work, kindly invited me to a session of the black caucus he was attending. When he introduced me to his mentor, she eyed me carefully.

"How do you identify yourself?"

"How do I—"

"I*den*tify yourself."

"Um, Italian Jew raised in Miami?"

"Well, then, you can't come."

Certainly it would be difficult to market myself as a white African Americanist. And certainly doing research as an outsider to any community is a challenge. But I do believe that in the end, it is the work that matters. I know that my own fears about my status as an outsider to the communities I study have diminished in proportion to the research and writing that I have done. Subject position and identity are important, but they do not define us entirely.

But I did grudgingly consider that advice, and to my surprise it actually opened up my research project and, I think, my research career. Instead of looking at black institutions exclusively, I decided to look at a range of alternative sites of rhetorical education, institutions that had been marginalized by previous histories. I discovered a variety of schools that also spoke to many of the same issues I hoped to address through my initial conception of the project.

For example, in addition to its variety of black colleges, Texas was home to the nation's largest residential women's college, Texas Woman's University, founded primarily through the efforts of public-minded Texas clubwomen who fought successfully for a companion school to the state's male-only Texas A&M. Though these women were often indifferent to suffrage and in many ways supported activities that may not appear sufficiently feminist to our contemporary eyes, they actively engaged in civic activities and promoted women's rights and expected women students to do so as well. Texas also had numerous vocational and teacher training colleges set up to serve first-generation college students in both white and black agricultural communities.

As I learned of these histories, I could not help but feel a kinship with the students at these schools. As a second-generation American and the first in my family to attend college, I have been steeped in the immigrant tropes of socio-economic advancement through education and familial pride in such achievement. I became determined to write histories that would not merely expand the body of historical knowledge in my field but also do justice to the diverse experiences of students and educators at previously marginalized institutional settings. Their histories are, after all, our own.

This project became my dissertation and, in its next incarnation, my first book, *Rhetoric at the Margins: Revising the History of Writing Instruction in American Colleges, 1873–1947*. In that work, I chose three colleges underrepresented by traditional histories: Texas Woman's University; East Texas Normal College, an independent teacher training school set up in explicit ideological opposition to elite liberal arts colleges; and Wiley College, a black liberal arts college in rural Marshall, Texas. I discovered that these schools, by emphasizing community uplift and civic responsibility and by validating local institutional and demographic realities, created contexts in which otherwise moribund curricular features of the era took on new possibilities, thereby fostering an ethos of public participation among their students.

At Wiley, poet and professor Melvin Tolson combined African American and classical rhetoric to produce a critical pedagogy that honored students' diverse voices and fostered progressive political action. At TWU, gender-based vocational education served progressive ends; unlike their peers at many contemporary women's colleges, students were encouraged to participate in public discourse, professional life, and politics. At East Texas, founder William Mayo held that each student had a sacred dignity that schools must honor and that practical universal education was the basis for a democratic society.

Moreover, each school's pedagogical approach was developed with local needs in mind, creating important differences and demonstrating once again the importance of taking local cultural and historical circumstances into context when developing pedagogies—and writing histories. For African American students and the emerging black middle class, for example, a classical education was seen as liberatory, the sine qua non of educational attainment.

As Tolson told his students, "Question everything. You are competing with students from Harvard and Yale" (qtd. in Flasch 19). In contrast, white women in Texas and in the South often had a much more conflicted relationship to the liberal arts, which they frequently saw not as liberatory but as limiting and belonging to an outdated antebellum finishing-school tradition, whose chief purpose, wrote one college president in 1874, "seem[ed] to be that of furnishing intelligent playthings for men possessing exhaustless wealth" (Kansas State Agricultural College 31). Each visit to an archive enriched my work, as each school illuminated the other.

Of course, I had no idea it would turn out this way at the start. The process of doing archival research is largely organic. Though we may apply a critical lens or favor a particular theoretical approach, the basic methodology of archival research remains the same: read absolutely everything and try to make sense of what happened. It is a bottom-up process and messy as hell—and, more to the point, scary, requiring faith that something will be found, even if it's not what you first went looking for.

With each of my institutional sites, the available material shaped the course of my research. Thus, with Wiley College, Tolson became the lens through which I examined African American rhetorical education. Though Wiley had little archival information available at the school, the enormous amount of biographical information I found on Tolson at the Library of Congress allowed me to focus on the question of individual teacher authority in the classroom; furthermore, his blending of rhetorical traditions allowed me to examine the question of how local, embodied pedagogies played against larger trends in African American and college education.

At TWU, the situation was reversed. I had very little instructional material from teachers, but I had a good record of institutional self-characterization through university publications and a wonderful record of student writing, with a near-complete collection of the student newspaper, yearbook, and literary journal. This source material allowed me to work backward from student writing to see what was institutionally valued and to examine how students themselves negotiated their identities as rhetors and public writers.

Discovering stories such as these are perhaps the happiest accidents of all. That these accidents come about only through painstaking research makes them no less miraculous. Chance may favored the prepared mind, but it is still chance. We never know where an archive will lead.

When I first began seriously digging into the archives, a senior scholar casually told me that I wouldn't understand what my dissertation was about until about three years after I had written it. I take the sentiment to suggest that scholarship is an ongoing process. One is never really finished. The work always leaves unanswered questions, which is actually a blessing. Unanswered questions are the fuel of the scholarly process.

Indeed, I have found that the questions that I couldn't answer in my dissertation have become the basis for my current research. The glaring limits of my ignorance have become the starting points for future knowledge. For example, I have been asked about the exceptionality of TWU: were other women's colleges similar, or did its particular historical and geographic circumstances make it unique? Yes, probably, to both. But this question has led me to a joint research project with another colleague on public women's universities throughout the South.

In researching Wiley College, I discovered that Tolson led a groundbreaking debate team that had a nearly uninterrupted string of victories against white colleges. His work with his team has led me to what I hope will be a book-length project examining the rhetorical and pedagogical role of debate and oratory in black colleges. Without intending to, I have come back to a variation on the project that began my research career. This time, however, I am prepared to do it.

And that's no accident.

Works Cited

Crawford, Robert, ed. *The Scottish Invention of English Literature*. Cambridge: Cambridge UP, 1998.

Flasch, Joy. "Melvin Beaunoris Tolson—The Man." Paper delivered during Black Heritage Week. Oklahoma State University, Stillwater. April 1967. Tolson Papers, Library of Congress.

Horner, Winifred Bryan. *Nineteenth-Century Scottish Rhetoric: The American Connection*. Carbondale: Southern Illinois UP, 1993.

Kansas State Agricultural College. *Catalogue*. 1874.

Miller, Thomas P. *The Formation of College English: Rhetoric and Belles Lettres in the British Cultural Provinces*. Pittsburgh: U of Pittsburgh P, 1997.

Thatcher, Rebecca. "106-Year-Old Huston-Tillotson Alumna Honored." *Austin American-Statesman*, July 29, 1999. LexisNexis.

2

Being on Location
Serendipity, Place, and Archival Research

Gesa E. Kirsch

For several years now, I have been studying the life and work of Dr. Mary Bennett Ritter (1860–1949), a physician, women's rights advocate, and civic leader active in California at the turn of the twentieth century.[1] During one of my trips to the Bancroft Library Archives at the University of California, Berkeley, I learned that being there physically, both in the archives as well as at the actual location where the historical subject lived, is invaluable. There were many things I would not have been able to explore virtually or on-line. It also helps to have serendipity on one's side, but that, of course, is not something one can arrange purposefully, although I am convinced one can be open to the possibility. In what follows, I briefly sketch the origin of my research project and describe what it means to walk in the footsteps of a historical subject.

> History nearly always begins as a simple curiosity about how we got here.
> —Robert Connors, "Dreams and Play"

I became interested in Ritter's life and work more than a decade ago when the archivist at the Scripps Institution of Oceanography (SIO) in La Jolla suggested I read her autobiography, *More Than Gold in California*.[2] In this well-written, lively volume, Ritter describes her quest for a medical education, her experiences running her own medical practice in Berkeley, her collaboration with other women physicians, her support of women students at the University of California, her contributions to the SIO during its founding years, her family's migration to California during the gold rush years, and the California scenery (which I have come to know and love during my twelve years of living in the state). After finishing the book, I was intrigued: What motivated this unusual woman? How was she able to move into the male-dominated world of medicine (being one of only two female students in her medical class)? What sparked her activism on behalf of women? How did she use persuasive and other rhetorical strategies to bring about changes she fought for so relentlessly (for example, she worked to improve minimum health and safety standards

for boarding houses and implemented sanitation guidelines for local dairies)?
Thus, I began my research to better understand the life, work, and rhetorical
agency of Ritter.

The archival materials I have been working with are limited. Some were lost
during Ritter's lifetime, a fact she recorded with regret in one of her diaries;
others are scattered across various archives because they are filed with her
correspondents, such as Phoebe Apperson Hearst, Ellen Browning Scripps,
and William E. Ritter, all of whom have collections in their own name. It is
interesting to observe that a single decision made by archivists—whose papers
are worth collecting under his or her own name—can greatly influence acces-
sibility and coherence of materials as well as the recognition accorded to an
individual's achievements and contributions to public life. As far as I can tell,
the main reason that any of Ritter's papers survive is because she eventually
married William Ritter, the first director of the SIO. Yet she lived an interesting
life in her own right, one worth restoring to the public record. The goal of my
project is to recover the contributions made by Ritter to public life, medical
history, and women's history by republishing her autobiography and several
articles that detail her strategies for advocating social change.

> Archival reading is . . . a kind of directed ramble, something like an
> August mushroom hunt.
>
> —Robert Connors, "Dream and Play"

My "mushroom hunt" began as soon as I arrived in Berkeley. Upon checking
in at the Bancroft Hotel (which I had chosen for its convenient location at
the edge of campus and its reasonable rates), I was surprised and delighted to
discover that the hotel's sitting room featured a small black-and-white picture
and brief mention of Ritter as part of a plaque commemorating the centennial
celebration of the University of California Prytanean Women's Honor Society,
of which Ritter was a founding member. It turned out that the hotel had been
the former women's club. Reading through several volumes of the Prytanean
Society oral history in the archives the next day, I learned that several early
club meetings had taken place at the hotel, where now biscotti and brandy
are served in the early evening. Staying at the Bancroft Hotel certainly was a
serendipitous choice and brought history back to life.

Upon discovering Ritter's portrait, I asked the hotel proprietor about the
plaque, its origin, and information about the Prytanean Society. He responded
with a phone number. This number led to an interesting series of phone calls,
whereby each member of the Prytanean Society I contacted suggested another
one with whom I might want to speak. During my stay in Berkeley, I spoke with
five different women, each of whom had new nuggets of information for me.

I learned about a speech given at the centennial celebration of the Prytanean Society that mentions Ritter prominently, and I was able to receive a printed copy of the remarks from the speaker. I was told about an article featuring the Prytanean Society's history that had been published in the *Chronicle of the University of California*, a journal devoted to the history of UC, in which Ritter was featured. I heard about the Prytanean Society's fund-raising efforts on behalf of the first university infirmary (and Ritter's involvement) and its continued support of medical facilities on campus. One Prytanean Society member suggested I check out the new Tang Center, which houses the University Health Services. There, on an early morning ramble, I located a conference room named in honor of both Ritter and Prytanean Society members. I would have neither suspected nor located this piece of living history without my "mushroom hunt" in Berkeley.

Once in the archives, I decided that my first order of business was to read through the Prytanean Society oral history volumes so that I would better understand the background of the women I had contacted. This choice was a good one; I got a clearer sense of university life for women students during the turn of the last century, the period during which Ritter had worked closely with students. My gaze thus shifted to the time period when Ritter had lived and worked in Berkeley. This new focus was helpful, particularly since the manuscripts I tackled next, the correspondence between Phoebe Hearst and Ritter, dealt with university life. Some UC women had demanded changes in student life and the curriculum during the 1890s, and they had solicited Ritter's help in implementing them. Women students had asked for greater access to the gymnasium, which required medical exams; Ritter had volunteered to provide these exams gratis. The students had also proposed setting up cooperative housing "clubs" to reduce costs and improve living conditions; Ritter had helped raise funds as well as solicited Phoebe Hearst's support for establishing these clubs.

The simple fact of being there, in Berkeley, walking across campus many times, jogging on the local trails, joining a campus tour, reading street and building names—all these activities made it much easier for me to read the handwritten correspondence and diary entries that prominently featured local places and events. Suddenly I understood what it had meant when a fire swept down Strawberry Canyon (I was able to decipher the name of the location and to comprehend the vastness of the disaster that had struck Berkeley), and I could picture the events organized by women students, such as a fund-raiser held in the "Faculty Glade" (a eucalyptus tree grove on campus that doubled as amphitheatre on special occasions), social gatherings in the Hearst Women's Gymnasium (which was financed by Phoebe Hearst and rebuilt by her son after it was destroyed by fire), or recitals held in the Greek Theatre (a big performance space that happened to celebrate its hundred-year history during my visit and was featured in a library exhibit, complete with pictures of women's performances). History came to life as I walked the streets of Berkeley.

Back in the archives, I had the great pleasure of meeting a man with whom I had corresponded for the last two years in preparation for my trip to Berkeley. He had been kind enough to look up sources and arrange for the microfilming and mailing of some material; he notified me of library hours and closings; and he understood the scope of my project. Now that I had arrived in person, he greeted me as an old friend and made sure I got the assistance I needed. For instance, when I inquired about photos and pictures of Ritter, he walked me over to the card catalogue (yes, the physical object, the wooden cabinet with drawers, still exists in the Bancroft Library), where original photos and portraits were catalogued (not all of them on-line yet); this search yielded a large charcoal portrait of Ritter I had not known about. I also learned that asking the archive staff about additional materials, sources, or suggestions was very helpful; their on-line search skills and knowledge of archival holdings were immense.

When I asked about a special issue of the *Chronicle of the University of California*, I was told that the journal editor's office, where I might be able to purchase a copy of the special issue, was several flights up in the same building. I met the journal editor and had a long, informative conversation about women's history at UC. I learned about Lucy Sprague, the first official Dean of Women at UC, who had followed closely on the heels of Ritter; about another book on UC women's roles as educators, schoolteachers, and curriculum developers (a copy of which I received gratis from the editor); and about the next issues planned for the journal, which included an invitation to contribute an article on Ritter. Climbing up a set of stairs that afternoon set me on a trail of materials I would not have expected nor been able to pursue virtually.

Reading the special issue of the *Chronicle* later that evening led me to further references that I could look up the next morning in the archives; for instance, I became acquainted with the early editions of the *UC Registrar*, a version of today's course catalogue, listing instructors, courses, and requirements. Here I could verify the years in which Ritter had served as the official medical examiner for women students and note changes in the curriculum, some of which were brought about by Ritter's work.

> Feminist archival research demands that we not only find lost women of the past but also become conscious of our positionality in relation to their positionality.
> —Jane Donawerth and Lisa Zimmerelli, "Dialoguing with *Rhetorica*"

I became aware of my own "positionality" when I came across an interview (part of the Prytanean Society oral history) conducted in the 1960s with a woman who had attended UC Berkeley in the second decade of the twentieth century. I was struck by how both interviewer and interviewee reflected the cultural values of their times when they discussed the topic of smoking among women: the older woman recalled the taboo about women smokers (only in private spaces); the younger woman spoke about how common it was to see women smoking in public places (during the 1960s). As a reader of the oral history in the new millennium, I could not help but observe how in our current day, smoking is neither very common nor very public among men or women.[3] This change in smoking habits, etiquette, and public policy during a one-hundred-year period served as a vivid reminder for me that cultural norms can change quickly and will always color the researcher's interpretation of archival materials.

In "X-Files in the Archive," Susan Miller notes that the premise, question, or hypothesis with which we start our research will ultimately determine what leads we pursue, what details we notice, and what claims we make about a person, historical phenomenon, or rhetorical problem. In setting out to do my archival research, my primary goal has been to find out more about Ritter's work, life, and accomplishments, but I also have to admit that I am fascinated by the things I first noticed when reading Ritter's autobiography—her determination to succeed, her "I-shall-keep-going-until-I-drop" attitude, and her feminist activism. At the same time, I try to resist too romantic a notion of this particular historical figure. I keep asking, What were Dr. Ritter's blind spots, prejudices, and preconceptions? What are mine? What were her racial, religious, and class politics? What are mine? How are these dynamics reflected in my reading of material and rendering of her life story? As Janet Eldred and Peter Mortensen remind us, archival research is, to some degree, always a nostalgic enterprise, a fact we need to acknowledge in our work. Liz Rohan further notes that we tend to select subjects we admire or with whom we identify over subjects we dislike or despise, and she recounts the ambivalence she experienced when studying a historical figure whose missionary goals were at odds with her own values.

One special challenge facing scholars working with historical materials, then, is how to create a space in which they can be respectful as well as critical of historical figures. That is, how do scholars present research subjects with respect and dignity when they may disagree with their values, attitudes, and actions? Anne Ruggles Gere cautions that historical figures—those who can no longer speak back—depend on the researcher's ethical treatment of their work. They have left behind many kinds of written artifacts, but it is the researcher's job to put these documents into a meaningful context. During her archival work on women's clubs, Gere "realized that these now dead and defenseless women depended upon [her] ethical choices in textualizing their interior lives" (214). Making appropriate ethical choices in representing Ritter's life is one of my most serious challenges.

> Perhaps it is that intensity and a return to childhood present-opening— the joyful moment of happy surprise—that makes me and others who work in the archives recall this process with a dreamy look.
>
> —Susan Miller, "X-Files in the Archive"

Two more stories of serendipity complete this narrative—"joyful moment[s] of happy surprise." Upon returning from my trip and catching up with e-mail, I received a message with the heading "Mary Bennett Ritter." I assumed it was from someone at the Bancroft Library following up on my many photocopy requests. But no, it was a message—out of the blue—from a great-great-niece of Ritter's. During that very week in which I was walking in the footsteps of my subject in Berkeley, she had done a Google search on Mary Bennett Ritter and found that I had given a talk at one of the Feminism and Rhetoric conferences. She told me that she had read "Aunt Mary's" autobiography and wanted to know about my scholarly interest in her relative. She is too young to remember Ritter herself but promised to look for any letters or photos her grandparents may have left behind. I cannot think of a more vivid example than this of bringing history back to life. It serves as a powerful reminder of a point Jacqueline Jones Royster raises: as scholars, we have an ethical responsibility to members of the community we study and, in the case of historical subjects, to their descendants, who have a right to the respectful and dignified treatment of their ancestors (272–78).

> The shortest route to discovery is lunch with an expert and telephone conversations with everyone you know in the field.
>
> —Jane Donawerth and Lisa Zimmerelli, "Dialoguing with *Rhetorica*"

Connecting with other scholars interested in Ritter herself or in the time period during which she lived has been very productive for me. Such connections have been made possible through papers I have delivered at national conferences, through informal professional networks, and through working closely with archivists. Each time I go to an archive or historical society, I ask the archivists I meet to share my interest (and e-mail address) with other scholars who might visit the archives. I find that networking and exchanging information about a common topic invigorates my work and leads to further insights. As I began composing these reflections on archival work—and here is my last story of serendipity—I received another unexpected e-mail, this one from a scholar who is planning to write a biography of Ritter's husband; we have already begun to exchange archival leads and plans for future work.

Notes

1. A version of this essay first appeared in *Peitho: Newsletter of the Coalition of Women Scholars in the History of Rhetoric and Composition*, 9.1 (Fall 2004): 1–5. I would like to thank the editors of *Peitho*, Susan Jarratt and Susan Romano, for encouraging me to write this essay and for granting permission to use this material here. Many thanks also go to Jabari Mahiri for hosting me during visits to Berkeley and for listening to my tales of archival adventures. I am especially grateful to Deborah Day, archivist at the Scripps Institution of Oceanography, University of California, San Diego, for introducing me to Ritter's autobiography, and to David Kessler, archivist at the Bancroft Library, University of California, Berkeley, for providing me with many archival leads.

2. My first trip to the SIO archives came out of curiosity about another woman, Ellen Browning Scripps, a major philanthropist in San Diego. Unable to find a biography of Scripps in local bookstores, I made my way to the SIO archives, where I met the archivist who shares an interest in women's lives and history and brought Ritter to my attention.

3. Massachusetts, the state in which I reside, passed a statewide smoking ban for all public places.

Works Cited

Connors, Robert J. "Dreams and Play: Historical Method and Methodology." *Methods and Methodology in Composition Research.* Ed. Gesa E. Kirsch and Patricia Sullivan. Carbondale: Southern Illinois UP, 1992. 15–36.

Donawerth, Jane, and Lisa Zimmerelli. "Dialoguing with *Rhetorica*." *Peitho: Newsletter of the Coalition of Women Scholars in the History of Rhetoric and Composition* 8.1 (Fall 2003): 4–6.

Eldred, Janet Cary, and Peter Mortensen. "Linking Reminiscence and 'Reality': Digital Possibilities in the Study of Nineteenth-Century U.S. Women's Rhetoric." Paper delivered at the Rhetoric Society of America. Austin, TX. May 31, 2004.

Gere, Anne Ruggles. "Revealing Silence: Rethinking Personal Writing." *College Composition and Communication* 53 (2001): 203–23.

Miller, Susan. "X-Files in the Archive." *Peitho: Newsletter of the Coalition of Women Scholars in the History of Rhetoric and Composition* 8.1 (Fall 2003): 1–4.

Rohan, Liz. "Sisters of a Common Cause: Evangelical Rhetoric in Two Turn-of-the-Century Female Authored Periodicals." Paper delivered at the Rhetoric Society of America. Austin, TX. May 30, 2004.

Royster, Jacqueline Jones. *Traces of a Stream: Literacy and Social Change among African American Women.* Pittsburgh: U of Pittsburgh P, 2000.

3

Getting to Know Them
Concerning Research into Four Early Women Writers

Christine Mason Sutherland

"The past is a foreign country; they do things differently there" (Hartley 3). Those of us who engage in rhetorical criticism of works of the past can testify to the truth of those words. We are strangers in the past: we have to find our way about, learn the language, understand the culture, and sometimes come to terms with a very different set of values. In making sense of the texts of the past, we face the constant danger of "presentism," a form of anachronism that treats our own contemporary values as normative.[1] There are a number of ways of dealing with this problem, or at least of minimizing its effects: these include studying the history of the period in some detail and reading as many works of that time as we possibly can.

But such rational means can be complemented by bringing to bear an alternative strategy, that of entering as far as possible into the physical world of our subject. This kind of holistic approach is consistent with the rhetorical method, which traditionally has looked beyond the rational to the emotional and the spiritual as means of persuasion. These elements are important not only in constructing discourse but also in understanding and evaluating it, and they are fundamentally bound up with the experience of the material and social world familiar to the writers we study. In thus attempting to experience the world of the past, we are in fact working with a different kind of meaning. Wes Folkerth makes the distinction: "[M]onothetic meaning is a function of the semantic component of sign systems such a natural language. . . . Polythetic meaning, on the other hand, is a 'time-immanent' mode of experiential meaning, meaning that is embodied in experience in time" (21).[2] Polythetic meaning, then, is derived from experience, in this case that shared experience that can bring us closer to the person whose writings we study, informing and illuminating our research. Closeness of this kind is especially associated with feminist practices, in which there is "a link between researcher and researched" (Bowles and Klein 17).

Getting in touch—as much as possible—with the physical context in which women writers of the past worked involves visiting the places where they lived. Much has changed, of course, since they were alive. But, as I hope to show, in some sense many of these women are still present in significant ways, even hundreds of years after their own lifetimes. In what follows, I discuss some of my own research into the physical, emotional, and spiritual contexts of four women writers—Lady Anne Clifford, Margaret Fell Fox, Mary Astell, and Dame Julian of Norwich—as a way of getting into closer touch with them and of attempting to experience, not merely read about, the worlds in which they worked. In the course of the discussion, I shall have occasion to refer to instances of another of the themes of this collection of essays: serendipity, the experience of which, though inexplicable (like Adam Smith's "invisible hand"), seems to be common among scholars.

Indeed, my research into the first of these women provides a particularly vivid example of it. In 1993, I was directing an honours student in her research into the autobiographies of seventeenth-century women. Our interest was particularly aroused by Lady Anne Clifford.[3] Lady Anne (1590–1676) is remarkable for the battle she sustained against her family in defence of her right to inherit the property of her father, a battle that continued for more than forty years. She had to contend not only with her uncles and her first husband (who wanted to reach a settlement allowing him to gain access to her money) but also with various legal advisors and even King James I himself. She defied them all. The diary she kept records her struggles—her distress, but also her determination not to give in. Eventually, the last remaining uncle died without heirs, and she did indeed receive the property she had all along considered to be rightfully hers. She saw this success as a vindication of her own resistance to the persuasion brought to bear upon her.

My student and I had been working on Lady Anne's diary throughout the year, but she was far from my thoughts when I took a holiday with friends in the Lake District.[4] One day we decided to drive into the charming little town of Appleby. As we walked up the steep main street, I suddenly caught sight of a bright garden full of flowers, just glimpsed through an archway. Now I, like Alice, cannot resist a garden,[5] so I plunged in, with no thought as to whether or not this might be a private residence. I found myself in a garden courtyard surrounded by little cottages. And out from one of them in the far corner came an old lady, leaning on a stick. I thought I was going to be warned off, told that I was trespassing. But instead she said, "Would you like me to show you 'round?" Quite by chance, I had happened upon the almshouse for elderly women founded by Lady Anne Clifford in 1651 in memory of her mother. The estate had been sold in 1961, except for one farm, whose income still supports the almshouse. And so the old lady showed us around the place, taking us into the chapel and explaining the various little rules, most of them laid down (so our guide said) by Lady Anne herself and still faithfully observed. They are read aloud to each incoming resident. One of them concerns laundry: the ladies are asked not to hang out their washing on Sundays, or on Wednesdays, when a communion service is celebrated. What I remember most clearly is the way our elderly guide talked about Lady Anne Clifford as if she had only recently died. "Lady Anne provided for . . ." "Lady Anne arranged that . . ." Obviously, the spirit of Lady Anne Clifford is still a living presence, and her work of charity goes on.

Another instance of experiencing the physical context—and one that again illustrates serendipity—I have already discussed in an earlier essay.[6] I summarize it here. It was 1999, and I was working in the archival library of Durham Cathedral, which holds a considerable number of the writings of Margaret Fell Fox (1614–1702). She is usually referred to by contemporary scholars simply as Margaret Fell because she is known to them almost exclusively as the author of *Women's Speaking Justified*, which she wrote while she was the widow of Judge Fell. However, much of her most important work, particularly her letters, was done after her marriage to George Fox, one of the founders of the Society of Friends, better known as the Quakers. After my stint in Durham, I went on to visit two sets of friends in Lancashire—friends I had not seen for thirty years. They knew I had been in Durham, but they did not know what I had been doing there. To my surprise and delight, each set of friends took me to places that were highly significant in the life of Margaret Fell Fox. First I visited Lancaster castle, where she had been imprisoned between 1664 and 1668. During her imprisonment, she wrote *Women's Speaking Justified*. Then I was taken high up on the fells[7] to "Fox's Pulpit," which is merely a large rock on which George Fox used to stand to preach. The remote venue was necessary because his preaching was at that time illegal. Later in the same week, another set of friends took me to a Quaker meetinghouse, built in 1673 and actually visited by Margaret Fell Fox herself in 1675. The building is surrounded by a peaceful cottage garden. There is no custodian, but a notice on the door welcomes visitors and invites them to use the small library and the kitchen (supplies provided) attached to the meetinghouse. Here, the virtues of the Society of Friends are palpable: hospitality, trust, gentleness, faith in both God and humankind.

I come now to the writer who is for me the most important of all the women I have studied: Mary Astell (1666–1731). A superb writer, famous for her eloquence in her own time, she is best known for her work in promoting women's education. However, as well as being an early feminist, she was also a philosopher and a political thinker, and in the early years of the eighteenth century, she engaged most successfully in political pamphleteering. I first discovered Astell by reading Ruth Perry's important biography of her, published in 1986. For some months I had been looking for a new research project, and on reading Perry's life of Astell, I realized I had found it. Astell's work appealed to me in a number of different ways: she was born in the seventeenth century, a period I had studied in some detail; she wrote from a Christian perspective, which I understood and valued; she was celebrated as a writer and recognized as a fine stylist, so my interest as a rhetorician was engaged; and she was significantly under-researched, so that I could foresee an opportunity of contributing something new to our understanding of the importance of early women writers. Accordingly, I applied for and received a research grant to study the works of Astell in the Bodleian Library in Oxford, since at that time—1988—hardly any of her works were available in modern editions. (Incidentally, on the topic of the physical, I think it is important to read early works in editions that would have been familiar to the authors. This physical contact with the books of the period is part of sharing their experience.) My particular project at this time was to make a study of Astell's style; but totally unexpectedly, I found myself reading rhetorical theory.[8] This was for me a major breakthrough. I proceeded to publish essays on her theory and practice and incorporated her into the curriculum of my course in the history of rhetoric. Then I moved on to other studies. But Astell haunted me: I kept coming back to her again and again.

My decision to write not just a few essays but a book about her was stimulated and encouraged during visits to London in 1999. During one of these visits, I took a boat trip on the river Thames. Mary Astell lived in Chelsea, close to the river, and must have known it well. Much, of course, has changed on the banks of the river during the intervening centuries, but much remains the same, for example, the Tower of London, with its Traitors' Gate opening on to the river, and the Chelsea Hospital and Greenwich Hospital (which I visited), both built by Christopher Wren in Astell's lifetime. Ruth Perry records one important historic occasion involving the river at which Astell may well have been present (298–99). It was July 1717, and a treat had been arranged for King George I. He was to proceed in the royal barge to Chelsea, where he would be entertained at a supper provided by none other than Lady Catherine Jones, the close friend and patron of Mary Astell. The occasion was a huge success. The king's barge was accompanied by another carrying musicians who played a set of pieces especially composed for the occasion by George Frideric Handel: the *Water Music*. The king was so delighted with the music that he had it played three times during that evening. It is quite likely that Mary Astell was a guest of Lady Catherine's on that occasion. At the very least, she would have been aware of what was going on and would almost certainly have heard the music, which was played on the river. Astell was a great lover of music and recommended it as recreation for the ladies in her proposed "Protestant Monastery" (*Serious Proposal, Part I*, 26). My trip on the river brought a strong sense of Astell, her interests, and her experience, and whenever I hear Handel's *Water Music*—which is often—I think of her as being present at its premiere.

A visit to a London church, St. Martin's-in-the-Fields, close by the National Gallery, provided a further insight into Astell's life. Every Sunday, Astell used to walk from Chelsea to hear a sermon preached there. The church itself, whose architect, James Gibbs, was influenced by Christopher Wren, provides a good metaphor for Astell's spirituality. It had been recently built in Astell's time and has none of the soaring quality of medieval churches. Rather, its balanced form strongly suggests all the best characteristics of the Enlightenment. Astell was a devout Christian who particularly valued reason; she saw no conflict between faith and reason, and much of her work is devoted to making clear the relationship between them. The very form of the church where she worshiped, then, bears witness to this partnership, and to meditate in the church, as I have done, is to bring oneself close to her in spirit.

The last person I shall discuss was the first woman to write a book in English: Dame Julian of Norwich (1352–1429?). Julian was an anchoress—an urban hermit. There were many such hermits at the time, perhaps as many as forty in Norwich alone. These were holy men and women who withdrew from the world to give themselves to prayer and meditation but also to serve the community by giving advice, especially on spiritual matters.[9] Julian herself is known to have given counsel to Margery Kempe of Bishop's (now King's) Lynn, another woman writer of the period. Typically, the anchoress (or anchorite, if a man) lived in a small cell with two or three windows. One window gave on to a room inhabited by a servant who would supply the daily needs. Another gave on to the street; through this the hermit could converse with those seeking advice. Julian's cell was built against the church of St. Julian and had a third window, this one giving on to the church itself, and through it she could participate in the services. Julian would have lived alone—except possibly for a cat, the only animal allowed to anchorites. Since her cell lay close to the river Wensum and the port of Norwich, she would have had to protect herself against rats, so it is quite likely that she had a cat, though she does not refer to one.

Little is known about Julian's life, not even her birth name: she took her name in religion from the church to which her cell was attached. But her book, a record of her visions, is one of the treasures of English literature. On May 8, 1373, Julian was gravely ill and thought to be dying. A priest brought in a cross, which he set at the end of her bed, and while contemplating this cross she received a series of sixteen "showings." When she recovered, she wrote them down and for the next twenty years reflected upon them. Then she wrote a second and much longer version, explaining what the visions meant: "Love was his meaning." Her *Book of Showings*, often referred to as *Revelations of Divine Love*, is a spiritual classic whose value has come to be recognized only during the last century.

Though most remote from me in time, Julian is the closest to me in sensibility and place, for I was born in Norwich. My father was born within half a mile of St. Julian's church and less than a mile from the site of Carrow Abbey, whose Benedictine nuns were responsible for Julian's cell. Some scholars think that she may at one time have been a nun there herself. The house built on the site of Carrow Abbey, and still known by that name, was later owned by the Colman family, for whom two of my great-grandfathers worked. When I was growing up, it could be hired for social events. We had a family reunion there, and one of my cousins used it for his wedding reception. We belong, in fact, to Julian territory, and she is part of the fabric of our lives. One of my school friends was named Julian after her (a spelling usually reserved for boys). Another wrote a play about her.[10]

But Julian is significant more broadly in the city where once she lived, and her influence still pervades Norwich and its people. Dead for nearly six centuries, she is now present again in Norwich in a new way. It happened like this: Julian's cell was pulled down at the Reformation, but the church survived until the Second World War, when, like many other Norwich churches, it was badly bombed and reduced to ruins. In the early 1950s, when the church was rebuilt, it was decided also to rebuild Julian's cell. The cell and the center close by now serve visitors from all over the world. It is staffed by Sisters from the Anglican Convent of All Hallows, Ditchingham, who have resumed Julian's work of providing spiritual support for all who visit there. I frequently visited the cell and the Julian Centre and library in the course of my research during my last sabbatical leave. Here in the simple cell, so like the one where she lived, it is possible to meditate and reflect, to reach out to her spirit and share her experience—an appropriate preparation for the study of her work I am about to undertake. The value of studying Julian in Norwich is underlined by Brant Pelphrey, who testifies to the difficulty of writing about her "far away from the unique atmosphere of spirituality and medieval history which are typical of Julian's Norwich even today" (11). And not only the history but also the artwork contribute to an understanding of Julian: there were several famous scriptoria in Norfolk at the time, and the fourteenth century is known as the East Anglian period of English painting (Lasko and Morgan 7). The artwork of the period is acknowledged to have influenced her style. Elizabeth Jennings believes that "she is in many ways more like a painter than a writer; she sees pictures and communicates them by means of language" (qtd. in Sister Eileen Mary, SLG, 7). At the very beginning of the Short Text of her *Revelations*, Julian refers to paintings of the crucifixion (125), and as Grace M. Jantzen suggests, her descriptions of biblical figures such as the Virgin Mary and Mary Magdalene may have been influenced by "portrayals of them in the painting and sculpture of the many churches and the cathedral in Norwich" (98). Many of these works of art are still to be seen in Norwich today, and part of my research involved the study of them.

What is interesting about these four women is that the work of three of them still continues: Lady Anne Clifford's almshouse survives, the Quaker movement bears witness to the labours of Margaret Fell Fox, and, as we have seen, Julian's work in Norwich has been revived. But what of Mary Astell? For over two hundred years, Astell was forgotten, but she is at last coming into her own. Since Ruth Perry published her biography in 1986, more and more scholars have become aware of her importance. Nearly all her works are now available in modern editions. My own book, *The Eloquence of Mary Astell*, was published in 2005, and a collection of essays on her work, *Mary Astell: Reason, Gender, Faith*, came out in March 2007. Her thought has great relevance for our own time, and I hope that she too will soon become a living presence again in our contemporary world.

Notes

1. Black rightly reminds us of the dangers of losing "historical perspective" (21). However, it seems to me that such loss is far less common than are the dangers of "presentism."

2. Folkerth gives credit for making this distinction to Alfred Schutz (Folkerth 21).

3. Excerpts from Lady Anne's diary and information about her are to be found in *Her Own Life*, edited by Graham, Hinds, Hobby, and Wilcox.

4. This is a particularly beautiful part of northwest England associated with the romantic poets Wordsworth and Coleridge.

5. Alice is continually frustrated in her attempts to get into the garden she glimpses through a tiny door. See Carroll, *Alice in Wonderland*, 15.

6. See Sutherland, "Feminist Historiography."

7. "Fell" is the term used of stretches of hills or moorlands in the north of England.

8. Mary Astell's rhetorical theory is to be found in her *Serious Proposal to the Ladies, Part II*, 117–52.

9. The best edition of the Middle English text of Julian's book is by Colledge and Walsh. Modern translations of the *Revelations* are also readily available.

10. Upjohn, *Mind Out of Time*.

Works Cited

Astell, Mary. *A Serious Proposal to the Ladies, Parts I and II*. Ed. Patricia Springborg. London: Pickering and Chatto, 1997.

Black, Edwin. *Rhetorical Criticism: A Study in Method*. Madison: U of Wisconsin P, 1978.

Bowles, Gloria, and Renate Duelli Klein, eds. *Theories of Women's Studies*. London: Routledge and Kegan Paul, 1983.

Carroll, Lewis. *Alice in Wonderland*. New York: Peter Pauper, n.d.

Clifford, Lady Anne. "Diary." *Her Own Life: Autobiographical Writings by Seventeenth-Century Englishwomen*. Ed. Elspeth Graham, Hilary Hinds, Elaine Hobby, and Helen Wilcox. London: Routledge, 1989. 35–53.

Eileen Mary, Sister, SLG. "The Place of Lady Julian of Norwich in English Literature." *Julian of Norwich: Four Studies to Commemorate the Sixth Centenary of the Revelations of Divine Love*. Ed. A. M. Allchin. Fairacres, Oxford: SLG, 1973.

Fell, Margaret. "Women's Speaking Justified, Proved, and Allowed by the Scriptures." *The Rhetorical Tradition: Readings from Classical Times to the Present*. 2nd ed. Ed. Patricia Bizzell and Bruce Herzberg. Boston: Bedford/St Martin's, 2001. 748–60.

Folkerth, Wes. *The Sound of Shakespeare*. London: Routledge, 2002.

Hartley, L. P. *The Go-Between*. New York: Stein and Day, 1984.

Jantzen, Grace M. *Julian of Norwich: Mystic and Theologian*. Trowbridge: Cromwell, 2000.

Julian of Norwich. *A Book of Showings to the Anchoress Julian of Norwich*. Ed. Edmund Colledge and James Walsh. Toronto: Pontifical Institute of Mediaeval Studies, 1978.

Kolbrener, William, and Michal Michelson, eds. *Mary Astell: Reason, Gender, Faith*. Aldershot, UK: Ashgate, 2007.

Lasko, P., and N. J. Morgan. *Medieval Art in East Anglia, 1300–1520*. Norwich: Jarrold, 1973.

Pelphrey, Brant. *Christ Our Mother: Julian of Norwich*. London: Darton, Longman and Todd, 1989.

Perry, Ruth. *The Celebrated Mary Astell: An Early English Feminist*. Chicago: U of Chicago P, 1986.

Sutherland, Christine Mason. *The Eloquence of Mary Astell*. Calgary: U of
 Calgary P, 2005.

———. "Feminist Historiography: Research Methods in Rhetoric." *Rhetoric
 Society Quarterly* 32.1 (Winter 2002): 108–22.

Upjohn, Sheila. *Mind Out of Time: A View of Julian of Norwich*. Norwich:
 Julian Shrine, 1979.

4

Making Connections

Alicia Nitecki

On the wall of my study at home hangs a head-and-shoulders photograph of a dark-haired, handsome man in his mid-forties wearing an army jacket and sitting in a car, leaning on his elbow. Wherever I am in the room, he appears to be looking directly at me and smiling. The photograph was taken in Munich in 1946, and the man in it is the preeminent prewar Polish graphic artist and publisher Anatol Girs.

I had first encountered the name Girs when, just as I was starting to write about Flossenbürg concentration camp where my grandfather had been incarcerated, a book with concentration camp stripes on its cover fell at my feet out of a box of old Polish books we had received from my husband's family. I noticed that the book, entitled *Byliśmy w Oswięcimiu* (We Were in Auschwitz) and dedicated to the Seventh American Army, had been published by one Anatol Girs under the imprimatur Oficyna Warszawska na obczyżnie (Warsaw Publishing House Abroad) in Munich in 1946 and had been written, as its publisher says, by three former concentration camp prisoners, Janusz Nel Siedlecki, Krystyn Olszewski, and Tadeusz Borowski, "shortly after camp Dachau-Allach was liberated by the 7th American Army."

This last name, Tadeusz Borowski, caught my attention because he is the author of the highly acclaimed—and highly controversial—stories about Auschwitz published by Penguin in English translation under the title *This Way for the Gas, Ladies and Gentlemen.* I had never read his work in Polish, nor had I had much serious scholarly interest in him. On reading *We Were in Auschwitz* closely, I realized that Borowski's famous stories in *This Way for the Gas* were not his later prose, as the Penguin edition and various critics give one to suppose, but his first and that Borowski's ideological stance on concentration camp existence, which has been repudiated or attributed to his "nihilism," was shared by his fellow authors and their publisher. I decided that the book as a whole, written so soon after the war and based, as Anatol Girs says in his preface, "on what the authors themselves experienced there and what they saw with their own eyes" and that reveals, as he puts it, "the pathological changes in the soul of these Europeans," should be made available in English and that I should translate it.

That decision led me down a scholarly road along which I discovered the actual reasons why Borowski was compelled to write his Auschwitz stories, stumbled upon a long-suppressed Polish work on the Holocaust, and reconnected with a person from my early childhood.

In order to translate *We Were in Auschwitz* and have it published, I needed to find the authors and publisher of the work to get their permission to do so. I did some research. I discovered that the first author, Siedlecki, had published an autobiography in English in 1994 and from it discovered that he was still alive and living in Yorkshire. I called him. He said he would be happy for me to translate their work. He had known Krystyn Olszewski from secondary school days in Warsaw, and they had met again in Auschwitz, but he had long lost touch with him, and he had had no contact with Anatol Girs for many years.

I deduced from reading a later short story of Borowski's, "The January Offensive" (included in the Penguin *This Way for the Gas*), that in it he is describing the actual circumstances under which he and his co-authors wrote their book. Because I had noticed some major discrepancies between the original Polish versions and the English translations of his stories, I tracked down the Polish language version of "The January Offensive" and concluded that the man whom he refers to in it as their "leader," whom he describes as "possessing an almost mystical flair for business . . . a holy man of capitalism, member of an influential and wealthy American sect spreading faith in the reincarnation of the soul, the self-destruction of evil, and the metaphysical influence of human thought on the actions of the living and the dead," and who, he says, had gone from Munich "to another continent . . . to Boston, the capital of his sect," was Anatol Girs.

I called the Mother Church of Christ the Scientist in Boston and was told that the last address they had for Girs was in New Hampshire. I found the name in the telephone book and called. Girs's daughter, Barbara, told me that her father had died in 1991, that in Munich after the war he had founded, and headed, the Family Tracing Service for Families, and that Borowski, Siedlecki, and Olszewski had worked for him there. Her father had brought some 9,000 copies of *We Were in Auschwitz* with him to the United States, but unable to sell many or to afford the cost of storage, he'd been obliged to destroy the whole run. She showed me the 1958 Warsaw re-issue of the book, inscribed by Olszewski "To you, Anatol, who are the father of this book," and Borowski's *Farewell to Maria* and *The World of Stone*, inscribed "To Anatol—the stories you made me write." Olszewski, she told me, was living in Warsaw, and she gave me his telephone number.

Barbara Girs also gave me letters Borowski had written to her father; in them, the formative role Anatol Girs played in Borowski's becoming a prose writer becomes clear. In one of them, the young man tells Girs about his plans and achievements in postwar Poland; gleefully reports that the translations of Hemingway and Saroyan that he had made for Girs in Munich were still the only ones of those writers in Poland; and says that Girs will be pleased with some stories he had been working on because "they express . . . your philosophy." In a postscript to one letter of October 1947, Borowski's wife, Maria, writes, "I am fully aware how much Tadeusz owes to you, and how much he developed both morally and intellectually under your care in Munich."

From reading the Polish biographies of Borowski and Girs, I learned that it had indeed been at Girs's suggestion that his three young friends spent their evenings in a "post-Hitlerite" Munich apartment in the summer of 1945 writing the stories for *We Were in Auschwitz*—in Borowski's case most reluctantly—and that their use of the first-person and their own names, for which Borowski has been both praised and lambasted by critics, had also been at Girs's insistence. "'They,'" Girs explained to his biographer, "is always someone else, not us."

My interest in writing an essay about Girs as the guiding light behind Borowski's prose and about the circumstances under which Girs had published the book led me to contact a woman living in the United States who had worked for him in Munich and had remained friends with his family. She told me that Girs had shared his bread with her husband in the camp, thereby helping to save his life, and that he had had a childish sense of humor—he called her "Pigówna" (Miss Piggy) until the day he died because, when she had first come to the Family Tracing Service, she had been so hungry she'd eaten sugar by the bowlful. I read the memoir she'd written about her family and, to my amazement, saw on the last page, among a list of names of her aristocratic relatives, the name "Count Żółtowski," a name familiar to me from my childhood.

As a Polish child growing up in England after the war, I found the language of Shakespeare more engaging than that of our own great poet Mickiewicz. I owe my ability to read Polish to a man whose life my stepfather had saved when they were being marched from a prisoner-of-war camp for Polish officers in German-occupied Poland to Lübeck in Germany and who, after the war, remained his closest friend. As a child, I considered this man the epitome of sophistication. Once when he was visiting us, he asked me, "Alicia, do you read

Polish?" Truthful nine-year-old that I was, I admitted I didn't. Every morning thereafter, for weeks on end, I sat on the kitchen counter laboriously reading out loud passages from the *Dziennik Polski* (The Polish Daily) to my mother as she bustled about her work. The man I so admired was married to a Mariola, Countess Żółtowska, I had spent many summers with them in London!

When I gleefully reported this coincidence to an older friend in Boston, she immediately responded that Żółtowska was the maiden name of a woman I'd once met at somebody's house and who had looked strangely familiar but whom I hadn't been able to place. I called the woman up. I had indeed seen her—one sunny morning in Mariola's house in London, many, many years ago. She is my Mariola's first cousin. We have since stayed in touch.

From Girs's biography, I discovered that during the Warsaw Uprising in mid-August 1944—the same time that my family and I had been taken from Warsaw to a labor camp in Schramberg-am-Rottweil in the Black Forest region of Germany—Anatol Girs had been taken to Auschwitz, from where, a week later, he was transported to the camp of Dautmergen, and it was there that he had first met Borowski.

Not being able to find Dautmergen on any map, I telephoned to ask Borowski's co-author, Olszewski, where it was. "I can tell you exactly—near Rottweil," he told me. Dautmergen—one of the seven so-called Unternehmen Wüste camps, established in mid-1944 to produce oil from oil shale—was situated at a distance of a very few miles from Schramberg, where I had been with my family. It was one of the camps my mother had in mind when she once told me not to be angry with the Germans in Schramberg; we had not been so badly treated. "The camps on the other side of Rottweil, however," she said, "were absolutely dreadful." And on reading one of Borowski's poems about Dautmergen, I realized, too, that those "divisions of Lancasters" flying across the sky and "writing freedom in smoke," to which he had "raised his head" and which he'd "greeted with his hand," were the very same ones that had made me as a three-year-old child in Schramberg bury my head and cover my ears with my hands out of fear. "What a small world!" I thought.

I did not yet know how small.

After my translation of *We Were in Auschwitz* was published, another translation project presented itself. A young woman with a scholarly interest in Borowski but no knowledge of Polish contacted me, asking if we could meet. She came bearing a large book, *Niedyskrecje pocztowe*, with a picture of Borowski on the cover wearing an army jacket, his hands raised in the air and a triumphant smile on his face—the same picture that Barbara Girs had given me, taken by her father in the English Gardens in Munich when Borowski was reciting one of his poems to him; it now also hangs on my wall beneath her father's picture. The young scholar asked me what the title meant. "'Postal Indiscretions,'" I translated, "'The Correspondence of Tadeusz Borowski.'" The volume was a collection of letters written by and to him from the time he was imprisoned in Pawiak and Auschwitz to 1951, when an unsigned telegram was sent to his parents after he committed suicide. The book included a number of letters from Girs, among them one in which he thanks Borowski for sending him *Farewell to Maria* and *The World of Stone* but disclaims Borowski's inscription, "The stories you made me write." "The stories I would have projected would have certainly been written differently," Girs states, adding in a fatherly-mentoring way, "Some of this gossip was not worth writing about," and, out of concern for Borowski's mental state, advising him to stay away from the camp theme for a while.

The book offered a compelling portrait of Borowski and of his relationship with Girs and an even more compelling picture of the Polish literary scene in the immediate postwar period. I began translating it for Northwestern University Press.

During the course of doing so, I was interested by a remark made by one of Borowski's co-authors in a letter to him written from Munich in September 1946. "Right now I'm reading Morcinek's *Listy spod morwy* (Letters from under a Mulberry Tree). The thing is written from a retrospective point of view, in the form of memories arising as a result of various experiences during a rest cure in the French Alps. . . . It equals in horrors, same ideological stance as ours . . ." Since that ideological stance has been seen by scholars of Holocaust literature as being peculiar to Borowski, I tracked the book down.

Letters from under a Mulberry Tree is a collection of twelve epistolary reflective essays in which the color of the Alpine sky and the bells of a French country church lead Morcinek back in one direction to the innocence of his childhood and the simplicity of his mother's faith and, in another, to the horrors of Sachsenhausen and Dachau. In its disavowal of any claims to "heroism" or "martyrdom" and in its unflinching portrayal of what existence in the camp revealed about human nature—"a psychologist would have wonderful material here to study and to deepen his knowledge of man," Morcinek writes—the work is indeed close in spirit to that of *We Were in Auschwitz*, as the letter I had read said.

Gustaw Morcinek, a forty-eight-year-old Polish Silesian Catholic, rural schoolteacher, and established prewar novelist and children's writer, had written *Letters from under a Mulberry Tree* in the summer of 1945 in Riviers, France. He had been arrested at the beginning of October 1939, taken to Sachsenhausen in December of that year, and then in March 1940 transported to Dachau, where he remained for the duration of the war. The work, one of the earliest on the Holocaust, had been published in the fall of 1945 in Paris and the following year re-issued in Rome and then in Poland. My research on it revealed that it is practically unknown today in Poland, having been suppressed after 1948 under Stalinism.

I decided to look for an American publisher for it, but first I needed to find the name of the copyright holder. The owner of the rights to Morcinek's works, I discovered to my amazement, is the son of a man who, like Girs, was a renowned prewar Polish master printer. I had read in Girs's biography his own amusingly sardonic account of a visit he'd paid to his estimable, older professional rival! The world, I thought, was small indeed.

I began to translate a few passages of *Letters from under a Mulberry Tree* to use in an essay about it and *We Were in Auschwitz*. As I did so, a Polish woman whom I barely know but who is familiar with my writing and translations called me saying that a friend of hers who had been in Dachau was trying to get compensation from the Germans, and she wondered if I knew anyone who had received it. On the spur of the moment at the end of the conversation, I said, "If your friend was in Dachau, ask him if he knew the writer Morcinek." An hour later, she called me back saying that his parents had, and she put her friend, Christopher Gabriel-Lacki, on the phone.

He and his father, he told me, had been taken to Dachau during the Warsaw Uprising. He had been fourteen years old at the time. His parents had been with Morcinek in the French Alps immediately after the war, and he had letters from him to them that he would bring to show me the next time he was in Boston. By way of conversation, and since I knew no one who shared my early childhood past, I said that I, too, had been in France after the war, in La Courtine and then in Nice. So had he.

A few days later, I remembered that once, when I had been looking through our family photographs from Nice, I had asked my mother who the other people in some of them were. "That boy," she'd said, pointing to a youth dressed in black swimming trunks and with a summer army jacket over his shoulders standing next to her, smiling and looking shyly down at the beach, "used to give you piggyback rides on the beach." I brought the box down from the attic.

When he next came to Boston, Christopher Gabriel-Lacki recognized my mother in the photograph immediately and identified her by name; my father, too, he said, looked very familiar to him. We had both lived on a street perpendicular to the Promenade des Anglais, both of us in the same house not far up it, on the left, the one with a brown door. He remembered hanging around with Polish children on the beach.

Neither one of us remembers it, but we both went on a pilgrimage to a miraculous painting of the Virgin Mary in the mountains somewhere not far from Nice. In the photo taken on that occasion, I am squatting on the ground at the front; Christopher is standing next to his mother, who is standing next to mine. The priest who is down on one knee at the lower left of the photo is the one I remember as having visited us in our apartment in Nice and whom Christopher identifies as being his parents' friend—the same priest, I learned from the letters Christopher brought me, with whom Gustaw Morcinek traveled through the French Alps and with whom he'd wandered around Nice for a few days at the end of 1945 before going on to Rome.

Christopher Gabriel-Lacki is now a graphic artist and professor of art. As a child, he had lived at 38 Smolna Street in Warsaw. At number 40 on that same street, Anatol Girs had had his art studio.

If the copyright holder gives his permission, an American publisher is interested in issuing Morcinek's book. I am going to translate it, and the man who, as a teenager, gave me piggyback rides on the beach at Nice is going to design the cover.

Anatol Girs is smiling.

Part Two

When Personal Experience, Family History, and Research Subjects Intersect

5

Traces of the Familiar
Family Archives as Primary Source Material

Wendy B. Sharer

In the last year of my master's program, my maternal grandmother suffered a severe heart attack—the beginning of a rapid decline that would ultimately lead to her death during my first year as a Ph.D. student. Only after my grandmother's death did I realize that her life experiences dovetailed with my interest in the critical reading and writing practices of politically active women. As Ronald Stockton suggests elsewhere in this volume, it is often a realization of mortality—a coming to awareness of the limits of life—that motivates scholarly research. My grandmother had participated during her lifetime in exactly the kinds of political literacy practices that fascinated me as a scholar, and yet I had missed the opportunity to learn from her about her participation in those activities.

What I Found in Grandma's Closet

Among the many scrapbooks, postcards, and photos that my family and I found in my grandmother's house after she passed away were programs, letters, and yearbooks from a variety of women's organizations in which she had participated. The materials included records of meetings and collaborative projects that were devoted to, among other things, reforming international affairs, studying political history, and advancing career opportunities for women. There were also programs from social outings, but these excursions were not, as I had mistakenly believed, the organizations' exclusive purpose. I knew that Grandma had been active within the Bethlehem, Pennsylvania, chapter of the Y-Dames (an affiliate of the YWCA), but I associated the organization with the rather mundane activities she participated in during her later years—activities such as preparing bags of roasted nuts for an annual Christmas fund-raiser. The Y-Dames were the "nut ladies" to me—I knew nothing of the international relations study groups or the letter-writing campaigns to improve local schools, both of which I found traces of in the cardboard boxes beneath Grandma's bed.

My surprise upon discovering these materials was followed by sharp disap-pointment. I had not learned about these or similar organizations in my many years of education, and I had missed the chance to talk with my grandmother about how she and so many other women used critical reading and writing practices to participate in active citizenship. The lessons I'd learned about the women's movement in American history had presented the period between 1920 and 1960 as a low spot or a lull—a time of stillness between two "waves" of women's activism. The documents from my grandmother's personal archives suggested something else.

I wanted to explore more traces of the practices I had stumbled across in my grandmother's house, in large part because I suspected that these practices were formative in her strong character, in the strong character she fostered in my mother, and—ultimately—in the strong character I credit my mother for instilling in me. Looking into the historical milieu that surrounded my grandmother's post-suffrage political activism, in other words, was a way to explore the origins of my own scholarly location. Through my mother, I had learned to study and critique assumptions about what was appropriate for me, as a woman, to do. Mom raised me by herself: my father succumbed to cancer when he was thirty years old, and my mother never remarried because she never met someone she thought would make a good father for my brother and me. As I grew up in a midsized northeastern city, I watched my mother combat the expectation that she would remarry quickly and the assumption that re-marrying would be the only responsible thing for her to do for her children. When she did not remarry, she faced questions from co-workers, community members, church families, and even the people she considered close friends. She was able to resist these expectations thanks largely to my grandmother's assistance in raising my brother and me. Grandma provided childcare so that my mother could work the multiple jobs she needed to support us and, later, pay for our college tuitions.

I also believe that my mother's ability to resist the powerful expectation that she would remarry derived from the self-assertive attitude she had witnessed in my grandmother, an attitude cultivated through Grandma's participation in women's organizations. A poem I found among my grandmother's belongings illustrates how work in women's organizations—such as the Y-Dames—fos-tered independence:

BOYFRIEND'S LAMENT
(To the Tune of—"The Man on the Flying Trapeze")

Once I was happy but now I'm forlorn
O how I wish I had never been born

Left all alone for to weep and to mourn
Betrayed by the girl that I love,

I plead for her love and I beg her to wed,
She joins a new club down at central instead.
They call her a leader, I call her misled,
Alas and alack—and alas
Now some weekends are sacred to cupid, say some
But not to this viper in skirts.
She goes to a conference stupid and dumb
And when I protest she says "nerts"—O—
She floats through the "Y" with the greatest of ease
She helps raise the budget because they say "please"
She won't give me dates though I beg her on my knees
That "Y" has blighted her love.

> —Song from the Volunteer Training Program,
> YWCA Y-Dames, Bethlehem, Pennsylvania

Much to the chagrin of their significant others, who were forced to take a backseat to the work of "the 'Y,'" women like my grandmother found in women's groups a channel through which to act independently in public matters. As this poem reflects, the Y-Dames were fully aware of the agitation they caused "their men," and they were bold enough to mock that agitation.

Where Grandma's Archives Led Me

Not long before my grandmother became ill, I had taken a graduate course on the New York Intellectuals in my master's program. The course focused on a group of avant-garde thinkers and writers in Greenwich Village in the 1920s and 1930s. In one of my weekly reading responses for that course, I expressed frustration with the overwhelmingly male construction of "the Intellectual." What, I wondered, were women doing at the time to address the political, ethical, and social issues facing the nation while these predominantly male "Intellectuals" and artists were debating politics and literature in Greenwich Village? Discovering my grandmother's materials brought this issue back to the forefront of my thinking, and I determined that my dissertation research would focus on this question.

The National League of Women Voters made perfect sense as a choice for the study of women's political rhetoric in the decades immediately after suffrage. When the Tennessee legislature ratified the Nineteenth Amendment in August of 1920, American women who had long labored for suffrage quickly discovered that although they could now cast their votes, the opportunity to do so existed in a restrictively structured, male-dominated partisan system. Women had waited on party politicians for decades—observing, agitating, protesting, and petitioning—while officially powerful literate practices (including the act of signing the Nineteenth Amendment into law) rested solely in the hands of male partisans. As a result, Carrie Chapman Catt, president of the National American Women's Suffrage Association, explained, "Many of us have deep and abiding distrust of all political parties" (18–19). Anticipating the difficulty of integrating former suffragists and their concerns into partisan American politics, Catt called for a successor organization to the NAWSA that would train new women voters in electoral procedures and further the interests of women within the platforms and administrative structures of political parties. This successor organization, proposed first by Catt in 1919 at the annual meeting of the NAWSA, became known as the League of Women Voters. The organization's goal, in addition to getting newly enfranchised women to vote, was to train women in the rhetorical tactics of American political influence.

The second organization I selected for research, the Women's International League for Peace and Freedom, enabled me to study the rhetorical efforts of politically active women in the diplomatic arena. When Dutch suffragist Aletta Jacobs learned of the cancellation of the annual International Woman Suffrage Association convention due to the difficulty of travel in wartime, she summoned various international women, including prominent American suffragists Jane Addams and Emily Greene Balch, to The Hague to discuss possibilities for ending male-run wars that interrupted progress toward international, universal suffrage. The women who gathered at The Hague in 1915 as the International Congress of Women for Permanent Peace—renamed the Women's International League for Peace and Freedom in 1919—expressed dismay about the antagonistic atmosphere of male-dominated international relations. Wars created by statesmen, Jacobs asserted, not only disrupted economic and social life but also halted the progress of women's rights by shutting down channels of international communication. Beginning with their first meeting in 1915, the founders of the WILPF sought to correct what they saw as fundamental flaws in traditional methods of international communication—flaws that led to militant nationalism, antagonistic diplomacy, and violence.

While I was able to discover some very useful overviews of the goals pursued by the LWV and the WILPF through published histories, I wanted to discover the specific practices and techniques by which both groups furthered their political efforts. I knew from published materials what the desired end results were, but I knew little about the means used to reach those ends. To find out more about these practices, I headed to the archives. While it would have been, practically speaking, impossible for me to go to all relevant archives, I decided

that I could find the most relevant materials by visiting three particular collections: the Library of Congress (which houses the papers of the National
League of Women Voters), the Swarthmore College Peace Collection (which
houses the papers of the U.S. WILPF), and the Schlesinger Library at the
Radcliffe Institute in Boston (which holds the papers of several key leaders in
both organizations).

All three archives presented challenges and immense benefits. My visit to
the Library of Congress challenged my patience—not because their staff was
not helpful but because so often the materials I requested had to be transported
from another storage building and, on several occasions, the boxes of materials
were not fully processed. I requested box after box of educational and publicity
materials and regularly had to wait for them to be delivered from an off-site
facility. But the waiting proved worthwhile. I discovered, for instance, an
impressive collection of educational skits and plays designed by the LWV to,
among other things, demonstrate the correct way to mark a ballot; illustrate
the most effective ways of testifying before a legislative committee; and comi-
cally highlight what *not* to do when speaking with a public official about his
stance on an issue of importance to women.

At the Schlesinger Library, I did not need to wait to get materials—indeed,
everything I needed was stored on-site. Much of the material, however, had
been microfilmed, and researchers, except in very rare instances, were asked to
use microfilmed records for their work. Anyone who has tried to locate specific
bits of information on a minimally indexed reel of microfilm knows how taxing this process can be. And yet, when I came across class notes prepared by
Grace Johnson, a leader of the Boston-area LWV and an English/composition
instructor at two junior colleges, I forgot about my stiff neck and the headache
I had developed while squinting at the microfilm images as they whizzed by
on the projection screen. I was elated to discover how clearly Johnson's class
notes reflect attempts to integrate political activism into an introductory level
English class. While her courses covered techniques of writing and speaking that could be applied to a variety of rhetorical occasions, Johnson was
particularly interested in training her students to perform as politically active
citizens. Her lecture notes on research writing, for instance, indicate her belief
that research involves discovering a topic with current political implications.
In a lesson on choosing and investigating a topic, Johnson recommended that
students consult government sources, such as state house records, congressional
reports, publications of government departments, and the U.S. census. Timely
and important topics, she advised, cannot be accurately identified from reading
popular media; rather, they can be found only in the primary documents of the
political process. Finding Johnson's class notes marked a watershed moment

in my research because they suggested that the historical recovery work I was engaged in was highly relevant to teaching practices in today's classrooms.

In the archives at Swarthmore, I found more ways to link the past and the present, particularly within the study and teaching of rhetoric. Perhaps the most awe-inspiring discovery for me was the records I found relating to U.S. WILPF founding member Julia Grace Wales. Wales, who was also an instructor of English at the University of Wisconsin, composed a booklet for the WILPF entitled *Continuous Mediation without Armistice.* The "Wales Plan," as the booklet came to be known, articulated the theory and groundwork for the kind of rhetorical machinery the WILPF sought to establish in the international arena. The proposal argued for the creation of a conference of non-governmental experts to discuss economic, social, and scientific aspects of international relations. More specifically, Wales called for the development of a conference of neutral nations to engage in a process of collaborative writing—to "come together in conference and endeavor to frame a reasonable proposition" that might resolve conflicts among belligerent nations. Leading experts from neutral nations would initiate the mediation process by circulating the proposition to belligerents, asking for feedback. With feedback from belligerents, the conference of neutrals would revise the proposition and resubmit it to the belligerents: "If the first effort fails, [the conference of neutrals] should consult and deliberate, revise their original propositions or offer new ones, coming back again and again if necessary, in the unalterable conviction that some proposal will ultimately be found that will afford a practical basis for actual peace negotiation" ("Appendix" 167–68). For Wales and the WILPF, "continuous mediation" meant "continuous revision."

Wales not only proposes the methods of collaborative writing for international mediation but also provides suggestions for what the new diplomatic genres produced through that writing might look like. For the document to be effective and convincing, she stresses, the writers of the proposition for peace should "append to it all conceivable arguments for its adoption, every possible appeal to the self-interest of every warring nation" (*Continuous* 4). The document must include rebuttals to anticipated objections and must be suitably geared toward the interests of the audiences it addresses. Additionally, a written request for feedback should be part of the genre so it appears not as an order but as an attempt to negotiate. Wales's instructions for rhetorical diplomacy mirror what rhetorical scholars today call "invitational rhetoric," or methods of communication that actively invite response.

I did, of course, hit some dead ends in my research. At one point while I was revising my dissertation and working toward its publication as a book, I traveled to the University of Wisconsin to see if I could locate any evidence that Julia Grace Wales had integrated some of the rhetorical ideas at the heart of the "Wales Plan" into the English courses that she taught. Much to my dismay, there were very few records from the English department at that time. I was able to find only a few course catalogues that mention Wales and an oral history collection tape in which the person being interviewed mentions Wales as a colleague in the English department. I had better success locating information about Wales when I consulted her papers at the National Archives of Canada shortly after my visit to Wisconsin, but still I could not find much that specifically related to her teaching career. Perhaps those records weren't seen as important enough to preserve. An archival researcher, however, cannot realistically expect the historical figure she is investigating to have kept everything, much less can she expect that everything her research subject preserved will make its way into official archival collections.

Why Grandma's Story Matters

A shortened version of this story about my discovery of an archival research project appears in the introduction to my book *Vote and Voice: Women's Organizations and Political Literacy, 1915–1930*. I included the story in the book because, at the time I was writing, I felt a scholarly obligation to do so. As I explain in that introduction, many historians have argued that writing history is not merely an exercise in the objective recording of factual information. Rather, it entails the careful selection and arrangement of historical traces from among an infinite number of possibilities. JoAnn Campbell has remarked that the writer of a historical account "is never a disinterested, objective observer of fact but always a selector of objects and interpreter of tales, [and so] the writing of history requires recognizing the location of the teller, the impetus of her investigation, and her vested interest in the tale" (305). The "vested interest" that propels historical investigation often involves feelings of admiration: "There is love here between writer, reader, and historical subject, and that love fuels the search for historical predecessors. As we articulate our individual relationships with the dead, we challenge writing conventions that would compartmentalize the history and historian, the text, and the love that produced and discovered the text" (308).

These points about the relationship between research and lived experience certainly resonate with me, and yet in my book I presented only a limited discussion of the vested interests and admirations that propelled my research. Quite honestly, I am extremely hesitant to mention these feelings and vested interests here. Isn't this, after all, a rather melodramatic story, the kind that might win an essay contest sponsored by *Lifetime* television—an idealistic young woman, raised by a single mother, earns a Ph.D. thanks largely to the traces of a politically active life left behind by her beloved grandmother? How can I turn this tale of my research as lived process into something "intellectual" and something "significant" for other scholars to read?

This dilemma is itself worthy of critical examination, and the process of interrogating the dilemma is, in my thinking, a useful endeavor for other researchers, especially researchers who are just beginning to consider archival or other historical research projects. Patricia Bizzell has suggested that scholars in rhetoric and composition "perhaps need more discussion of the part played in the setting of scholarly agendas and the constructing of scholarly arguments by our emotions about research topics" (12). I agree. In fact, I suggest that we seek out and celebrate the role that our emotions play in our selection of research projects. In the process of writing my dissertation, my book, and, most recently, this article, I've been focusing on "acknowledging" the part my emotions and experiences played in the construction of my research agenda. The focus, in other words, has been on making sure that I've responsibly revealed my biases and my locatedness as a researcher. This business dispensed with, I've tried to move on to "scholarly" analysis. As a graduate student formulating a dissertation project, I spent a great deal of mental energy debating the validity of my ideas—thinking, as I did before writing this piece, that the details of the origins of my project are best suited for a "nonscholarly" arena. How I came to this project, I thought, is too "smarmy" (read: affective and serendipitous) to make that journey respectable to or instructive for other researchers.

Yet my most significant (to date) research project originated within the emotion-laden family and life experiences that preceded that research. Don't these origins, then, deserve celebration rather than brief, and somewhat apologetic, acknowledgment? I want to suggest that, rather than turning away from or hesitating to reveal how research is connected with lived, and often affective, experiences, researchers should seek out these experiences and make them known in a spirit of enthusiasm. I hope that, as someone who now advises doctoral students, I can encourage new scholars to find topics via their lived experiences, because those experiences help us to recognize what is significant, even if we are not able to articulate a rational, "neutral" reason for that significance.

Of course, I'm not suggesting that we omit the process of thinking critically about what we select and what we omit in our setting of research agendas. I'm simply suggesting that we look favorably on and in fact encourage affective connections to our research projects. I urge researchers not to dismiss the inspirations that they cannot fully articulate as part of a rational effort to locate themselves as researchers. I hope that, by presenting my story, I can foster a desire in future scholars to explore the rhetorical practices of family members and friends and, at the same time, to counteract the restrictions and assumptions that place family and friends—"personal relationships" and the affective domains that surround them—beyond the boundaries of valid research.

An added benefit of raising the scholarly standing of the affective domain in research might be the expansion of archival resources for the field. As I have argued elsewhere, what gets preserved in archival repositories is often that which is already deemed significant. The materials hidden under the beds and in the attics of friends and family might not, thus, seem appropriate for these collections. Yet these records—produced and contained within the lived experiences of our friends and family—are valid, and potentially enormously influential, sources for historical and archival scholarship. I encourage other scholars to seek out records like the ones I stumbled upon. I assumed that no such records existed, and it did not cross my mind to look for them, because this was, after all, "just" my grandmother. My relationship with her was part of my "private" life. Now I wonder what more I might have learned if I hadn't been blind to the possibilities for research in that life.

Works Cited

Addams, Jane, Emily G. Balch, and Alice Hamilton. *Women at The Hague: The International Congress of Women and Its Results.* New York: Macmillan, 1916.

Bizzell, Patricia. "Feminist Methods of Research in the History of Rhetoric: What Differences Do They Make?" *Rhetoric Society Quarterly* 30 (Fall 2000): 5–18.

Campbell, JoAnn. "Afterword: Revealing the Ties That Bind." *Nineteenth-Century Women Learn to Write.* Ed. Catherine Hobbs. Charlottesville: UP of Virginia, 1995. 303–9.

Catt, Carrie Chapman. *An Address to the Congress of the United States.* New York: National Woman Suffrage, 1917.

Sharer, Wendy B. "Disintegrating Bodies of Knowledge." *Rhetorical Bodies.* Ed. Jack Selzer and Sharon Crowley. Madison: U of Wisconsin P, 1999. 120–43.

———. *Vote and Voice: Women's Organizations and Political Literacy, 1915–1930.* Carbondale: Southern Illinois UP, 2004.

Wales, Julia Grace. "Appendix A: International Place for Continuous Mediation without Armistice." Addams, Balch, and Hamilton 167–71.

———. *Continuous Mediation without Armistice.* Geneva: WILPF International Office, 1916.

6

The Biography of a Graveyard

Ronald R. Stockton

There is a small town deep in the hills of southern Illinois with the odd name of Sesser. Tradition says it was named after the government official who filled out the incorporation papers a century ago. The area was first settled in the 1820s by people mostly from Kentucky, North Carolina, and Tennessee. (The Native American population was concentrated along the Mississippi and Ohio rivers, not in this inland county.) Almost all of these early settlers were white and Protestant, mostly some form of Baptist. For the first few decades of the century, burials were on farms. It was not until 1840 that anyone created a formal graveyard. It was called Horse Prairie, named after the area where it was located, and lay just next to the Baptist church of the same name. It was the burial place of choice in the township for the next seventy years, until the city was incorporated and produced a public graveyard. By that time, the coal mines had opened and workers had begun to pour in. Many of the new arrivals were from Italy and Poland and brought their Catholic religion with them, so the public cemetery became their preferred burial place.[1]

How I came to be the biographer of Horse Prairie Cemetery is a surprise even to me. By profession I am a political scientist, trained empirically. Graveyards are not something that political scientists ordinarily study. The fact that my specialization is nonwestern political systems puts me even further from the topic. Maybe it has something to do with a generational process. A colleague who studies these things says that when we reach a certain age, we often begin to sense our own mortality and to reflect upon our heritage and what we will leave behind. Somewhere in my fifties, I got interested in genealogy. At that point in my career, I had published two books, had been department chair for two terms, had won the Distinguished Teaching Award, had fought the obligatory academic wars, and was very comfortable in my skin. I had headed some professional associations and felt that in my career—which was far from over—I had achieved everything I had hoped to achieve. In 2000, when my second book came out and I had nothing on my To Do list, I discovered the Mormons' genealogy list on the Internet and suddenly realized there was a wealth of information out there for people like me to find.

But let's step back for a minute. Not everything begins when a person hits fifty. When I was nineteen and a student at Southern Illinois University, a professor—Dr. Ridgeway—stopped me after my class in Illinois government and asked if I knew anything about my family history. I said I knew little except that we had come to southern Illinois from Kentucky a century before. The professor told me she had been doing research on her own family and had run into relatives named Stockton. She said if I could find the names of my family four generations back, she might be able to tell me some things about them. Ridgeway thought we might have been Quakers at one point, something I had never considered. I made a few efforts to find out some names but never really followed up on that offer. Still, I was intrigued with the idea that it was possible to learn about ancestors whose names I had never heard. What an idea to put into the head of a nineteen-year-old! We who are faculty often don't realize the impact we can have on students outside of the classroom. A kind word or a subtle suggestion can sometimes germinate for years and then bloom. Dr. Ridgeway has been gone for decades, but that seed she planted has continued to germinate.

I had always been interested in my family history but had never been able to get much information out of my parents or grandparents. Partially it was the culture. Many people who went to the interior of the country in the 1800s left behind their past and the stories that past contained. They were starting anew in a new land and often had memories they wanted to forget. They were also poor. Some could not read or write, and those who could did not sit around writing diaries after a long day in the fields. They lived their lives, bore their young, buried their dead, and marched through history without leaving much of a footprint.

Partially the problem was me. Like so many young people, I never took the time to find out about the past. Like so many other people with gray hair, I wish now that I could have just an hour with those people I knew as a child so I could ask them the questions that will remain forever unanswered. I would ask my maternal grandmother why our family left France and how it felt to a young girl to set off for a new country. I would ask my maternal grandfather to tell me about his father, who had fought in the Civil War and been involved in the siege of Atlanta. Did my great-grandfather ever say what he thought of General Sherman or how he felt when he heard that Lincoln had been shot? On the paternal side, I would ask my grandmother to tell me what she remembered about her Lewis grandparents and whether it is true that we are descended from that famous Virginia family. And I would ask my great-uncle to tell me about his parents, my great-grandparents. Unfortunately, these are questions that can never be asked. But fortunately, some questions *can* be answered with genealogical research. In just three years I was able to find Civil War records, early land records, shipping records, and family histories that other branches of the family had compiled.

The Search for Ancestors

My first big discovery was of my great-grandfather who had participated in the Civil War. I knew Nathan was from Indiana but did not know much more. My grandfather was the last of Nathan's children, and both men died without leaving much by way of family stories. The Indiana census records of 1850 were a windfall, since all names were indexed. It is hard to say how exciting it was to find my great-grandfather as a little boy with his parents and baby sister on a small piece of land in the middle of the state, then to find the marriage record of *his* parents and realize that there had been a brothers-sisters double marriage in which Henry had married Nancy at the same time that Henry's brother had married Nancy's sister. What was less thrilling was to read about how that county was freed up for white settlement by the evacuation of Native peoples from central Indiana (Cayton). To me, my family was made up of frontier people who broke the land and created a state. But every heroic event in history has an asterisk.

Much later, I found Nathan in the 1860 census, just a year before he joined the Union army. He had been misidentified in the index and I found him by accident, a farm laborer living next to a Miss Bradford, several years younger. That dignified lady in the family photograph that we had known as Catharine Henretta was here listed as "Kate." That simple discovery was one of the thrilling moments of my genealogical quest, to realize that my great-grandfather had called my great-grandmother Kate.

Somehow, each of these details linked me with those who had gone before and let me know something about their lives and, in a sense, about my own, who I was, and where I originated. Not everything was to my liking. A fact of my antebellum Kentucky ancestors was quite disturbing. I was not so naïve as to think that my paternal family had been spared the poison of racial thinking, but I knew they had been poor farmers and had not likely owned slaves. I also knew that they had supported the Union and that some had been persecuted in that dangerous border area for their loyalty. It was an unsettling surprise, then, to find in an 1840 census record that one of those ancestors had in fact owned four slaves. I could not even imagine why someone with so little land would have four slaves. If finding my great-grandmother Kate was a high, finding my great-great-great-grandfather John with four slaves was a definite low.

The Graveyard Project

The graveyard project was a natural outgrowth of these interests. As I discovered information about each ancestor, I wrote it up in a short "Family News Note" and sent it out to relatives. They were pleased to get these missives, but in a sense this information was of interest only to those in the family. Genealogists tend to be self-involved by nature and are not often interested in what other genealogists are finding unless it relates to their own family. Facts accumulate, but there is no history in a sense of learning what had happened and why.

My own approach is somewhat different. I realized early on that the amount of factual information I would learn about ancestors would be relatively little: the names of forgotten ancestors, where they were born, how much land they owned, where they lived in a given census year. I decided that the way to learn about my family was to learn of the times in which they lived and of the historical processes underway in their age and place. If they moved, what other people were moving at the same time, and why? If they were in a given place at a given time, what do we know about that place at that time? When I learned that my French immigrant great-grandfather had served in the French army in Madagascar, that set me off on a search for French colonial and military history. Why were the French in Madagascar, and what would my great-grandfather's life have been like? Again, there were those disturbing asterisks.

In 2001, I had a sabbatical and decided to spend part of it in genealogical research. My parents were in their upper eighties at the time, so I wanted to do something in their honor. That hometown graveyard came to mind. Genealogists often make lists of people in graveyards for the historical record. These can be published in small booklets or even put on the Internet. Often they include names, dates, gravestone inscriptions, and sometimes even photographs of gravestones.

Horse Prairie Cemetery had 829 graves at the time. In my youth, I had visited it every Decoration Day (as Memorial Day was then called). We would put flowers on the graves of our relatives and visit with others who were doing the same thing. In a town of 1,500, everyone seemed to know everyone else, and many of us were related. My grandparents were buried there, as were my great-grandparents and other relatives. My dad's baby brother was there, who died when he was four, and my dad's uncle, our town's only fatality in World War I. That place would always be filled on Decoration Day, with people from the town coming to pay homage to their families and their memories. My dad regularly made a donation to the graveyard association for the maintenance of the grounds.

In typical southern Illinois style, my parents, while in their sixties, had purchased their own gravestone and left it sitting in the cemetery expectantly with their names and birth dates; only the closing dates were left empty. It was a bit odd to see the gravestone of my living parents, but it was the custom of those provident people to prepare for the inevitable. It is rather healthy when you think of it, acknowledging that which we all know will come.

My plan was to drive the five hundred miles south from Detroit to Sesser and to make a list of the graves. My first step was to make sure that the minister of Horse Prairie Baptist Church (fifty-nine members) would be comfortable with the project. We met, and he liked the idea. He even volunteered a couple of older members who could fill in some details about the history of the place. He did note that although the graveyard abutted his church property, it was not controlled by the congregation but had its own board of trustees.

One very hot week in May, I spent three grueling days in the graveyard making a list of all the names on the stones. I also recorded all the poems, scriptures, laments, and other stone writings that I could read. When it was over, I went back to Detroit with burned skin and an aching back to enter the information into a Word program that could be turned into a pamphlet at some point. In a couple of months, when my wife, Jane, had a break, we went back to the graveyard together to check the accuracy of my entries and to fill in the missing details. Fortunately, Jane had an uncanny ability to read faded poems and inscriptions, so this produced a much-improved list. A second development then arose. When I showed the draft list to my aunt, she asked, "Have you shown this to Clara Brown?" She explained that Clara had earlier published a list of people buried in the public cemetery and might have some information on Horse Prairie Cemetery as well. The next day, Jane and I met Clara, a delightful farm lady in her eighties. Not only had she made a list of Horse Prairie graves about two decades earlier, but she had used her rich connections in the town to fill in missing details and to locate genealogical and family information on many of the persons buried there. She had also gone to city records and graveyard records and had identified graves without gravestones or that were otherwise unknown. Her diligent research had added scores of graves to the list I had compiled.

As I looked over her list, I realized that this was a document of some historical significance, at least to those people whose families were in this place. Clara had been able to locate family historical records (parents, spouses, children, siblings, circumstances of death) for nearly seven hundred persons. Many of these details would be lost within a generation if they were not somehow put into the historical record. I suggested that we combine our efforts. Clara had circulated her list in a small genealogical newsletter but had not otherwise made it available to genealogists and local historians. I offered to take her working draft, update it with the additional names I had recorded from the past twenty years, and add in the poems and inscriptions I had recorded. I said I would produce a book of the result with her as first author. Amazingly, she agreed on the spot and turned her complete file over to me.

Producing the book took three years and a lot of work.[2] The manuscript was in rough form and had to be polished. I also decided to transform it from a simple list of genealogical and family records into a more comprehensive book by adding supplements and aides for the reader: a schematic map of the graveyard, a list of terms and phrases to help understand the graveyard and its culture, an index of names with the location of the graves, and several nostalgic poems about graveyards, death, and reflection (such as Abraham Lincoln's haunting poem of his return to his hometown after twenty years). I also put in an academic article I had written for the *Journal of the Illinois State Historical Society*. The preparation of this article, "Death on the Frontier," is a tale of its own. I was very apprehensive about submitting an article to a history journal. Historians are very serious about their craft, and it did not seem wise for someone not trained in their methodology or their sources to think his findings would be worthy of a professional journal. Fortunately, two colleagues (Gerald Moran and Marty Hershock) proved very supportive of my efforts, offering suggestions and sources that only historians would have known. They transformed my effort into an article of interest to professional historians.

Death on the Frontier

When I first got back to Detroit with my initial list, I noted that 683 of the names had both birth and death dates. I decided to enter that information into an Excel database to create an index of names and also to see how death patterns changed across time and whether there was a gender effect. Viewing these 683 people as individuals did honor to them as persons and was of great interest to their families and will be to future generations, but it would be of little interest to anyone outside of that small circle. Reconceptualizing those obscure individuals as a sample of frontier people whose community had evolved over time put them into a historic context of broader interest. In a sense, individual stories, taken in aggregate, became history with a capital *H*.

I broke the burials into decades starting in 1840 and stretching until 2000, sixteen decades in all. My primary interest was in the 365 burials in the nineteenth century. This was the time that most corresponded to the "frontier" period of Illinois history. Most of those people had either settled the land themselves or were the children of those who had. Using their death records to compare their lives with the lives of those who came after them could be interesting.

My research produced four major findings, all of which had to be checked against other data to confirm their reliability. My first finding was the most shocking: of those graves of the nineteenth century, a full half were for children under ten, a majority of whom died within a day of birth. In the last half of the twentieth century, by contrast, it was very rare for a child to die (only one infant burial of 176 after 1965, for example). Everyone knows that life in those days was dangerous, but these figures were stunning. When I checked standard histories of that era, I found that the Horse Prairie data were only a little higher than average. These figures were clearly within a confirmable range of frontier life and death.

But not everything is numbers. At the root of these statistics are human beings. When I reflected upon the numbers in terms of human experience, I realized how different a funeral is today from what it had been in the 1800s. For us today, a funeral is often of a venerated elder, someone who had a long and fruitful life. Often the ceremony is an occasion of celebration with grandchildren and great-grandchildren in attendance. But that was not true in the nineteenth century. Most funerals were for young children who had not even had a chance to establish themselves or define who they were or what they would be. When I talked to Clara about this finding, she noted that almost all of the unidentified graves were probably infants who died soon after birth.

In honor of those who died young and of those who had to give them up, I included in the poetry chapter the moving "Prayer for a Very New Angel" by Violet Alleyn Storey. In it, a mother briefs God on how she cared for her daughter: she wet the brush to curl her hair, kissed her on the left cheek in the morning, and left a light on at night. In a prayer that sounds hokey today but would have resonated with mothers a century ago, the mother in the poem asks, "Just, just tomorrow morning, God, I pray, / when she wakes up, do things for her my way" (Brown and Stockton 109).

On the opposite end of the age scale, I discovered that very few of those buried in the nineteenth century were in the older age brackets. Of all burials in the 1800s in Horse Prairie Cemetery, only seven were of people seventy years old or more. By contrast, in the last fifty years of the twentieth century, over 60 percent were seventy or more. Since the reality of child death did not stop survivors from reaching a ripe old age, something else must explain the small number of elders. When I turned to the census records, I found the answer. There were just not many elders around. In 1840, to take one example, only 11 percent of the county population was forty or older, and in the whole state, only 2 percent were above forty-five. Today we forget how new our country really is and how unique the frontier experience was. In 1840, Illinois was "the West," the place where young people went to start a new life.[3] Older people are not in that graveyard because there were so few older people "out west." Living in Illinois was something young people did, not their elders. As someone whose small grandchildren consider Camp Grandma and Grandpa their favorite place, I felt a sense of loss for those children.

Regarding gender, it turns out that there are 17 percent more men than women in the Horse Prairie graveyard. In the early decades, this may have been partially due to the fact that the "frontier" simply had more men than women. (In 1840, there were 117 males for every female in the state.) But when I looked at infant deaths, I saw the pattern confirmed. Among infants under one year of age, there are thirty-one boys and twenty girls, a ratio of 1.55. From ages one through five, the numbers are fifty-two and thirty-nine, or a 1.33 ratio. Since small children would have been born in Illinois and would have had a "normal" gender distribution, there was clearly some risk in being born male. I could find no explanation for this pattern other than to note that even today, childhood is more risky for boys than for girls.

Finally, I confronted a puzzle. In a cemetery with a disproportionate number of males, females dominate among those between sixteen and thirty-nine years old. There are fifty-two females and thirty-eight males in this category, a ratio of 1.37. I immediately assumed that this pattern was linked to the dangers of childbearing, but there was no such easy answer. For example, the balance shifts back toward males for those in their forties, where women might have had an even higher risk in pregnancy. Likewise, the county's census mortality schedules for 1850 and 1860 (listing those who had died in the previous year, 158 in all) contradict the pregnancy hypothesis. Most people died from the big killers of the age: various fevers (scarlet and typhoid being most common), whooping cough and croup, dehydrating conditions such as diarrhea and cholera, and lung conditions such as pneumonia and tuberculosis. Only three women died from conditions obviously linked to childbirth or pregnancy. How do we explain these contradictory data?

One factor may have been the rapid decline in fertility (the number of children born per female). Carl Degler, who has written the definitive work on this subject, found that for white women, this decline was 50 percent between 1800 and 1900. He calls this "the single most important fact about women and the family in American history." He also found that the decline was steeper for rural areas (including "newly settled regions") than for urban or small town areas (181–82). As to why this occurred, he suggests that the shortage of land and the "close-knit family, held together by ties of affection," caused parents to have smaller families so that their children would not have to move away as they had done. Obviously, a woman bearing five children would have less risk than one bearing ten. Put simply, affectionate families saved women's lives.

Of course, there are other possibilities. One is that the high number of female burials balanced out the high rate of boy deaths and there was no female spike at all. It is also possible that a postpartum mother would be more at risk in the event of an attack of croup or some other debilitating condition so that pregnancy-related deaths are concealed under other categories. Likewise, women—as the primary caregivers—might have been more exposed to contagious conditions such as whooping cough than males. But none of these possibilities is definitive. In the end, we are left with more questions than answers but also with a profound awareness that explanations are more complex than we anticipate and that what we expect is not always true.

Final Thoughts

We scholars, with our models and theories and data, often fail to acknowledge that research is a very personal activity. Many of us are reclusive by nature, going off alone to do our research and write our books and articles. But the costs of an academic life are considerable. To set off on a two- or three-year project requires a serious commitment of time and psychic energy. Without passion, it would be hard to do what we do. A colleague once asked if I had ever written anything of a personal nature, and I said, only half in jest, "Everything I write is autobiographical." This may seem a strange comment for a person who writes on public opinion and comparative politics, but in a sense we are driven by our passions. We often choose topics because they interest us, because we are excited about the subject and what we might find. At the same time, passion and personal interest are not enough. Without the tools of our trade—our methodological skills, our scientific training, the theories and models that help us shape our research and analyze our findings, the rules of validation and confirmation that constrain our preferences and discipline our conclusions with science—we would not be able to make the contributions we make. Without the personal impulse, much that is achieved would not be achieved, but without the science, much that is achieved would be of limited value and would not enter the realm of scientific knowledge. I was able to turn a family genealogy project into something of interest to the broader scholarly community because I subjected my analysis to academic discipline.

Three comments on this project gave me exceptional pleasure. In combination, they capture what I am trying to say. An anonymous historian who reviewed "Death on the Frontier" for the *Journal of the Illinois State Historical Society* commented that the article showed a good use of historical data to contextualize the Horse Prairie graveyard and as such makes "an important contribution to the study of frontier history." Second, a retired historian from Southern Illinois University who was professionally active in the study of the region's history noted that the footnotes were very informative and the statistical patterns very revealing so that the article could easily have been published by a national rather than a state journal. That was high praise. Finally, when Clara Brown was interviewed by the local newspaper after the book came out, she said, "I thought he would just produce a list of names. This is a real book." That was the best of all.

Notes

1. There was, and is, no Catholic graveyard in Sesser.

2. Books such as this are of no interest to commercial publishing houses. I was able to find a private publisher who would produce 150 hardbound copies on acid-free archival paper. After giving copies to my relatives, I sent copics to major genealogical and local history research libraries and donated others to the Genealogical Society of Southern Illinois, a local history society with an extensive publication list, and to the Goode-Barren Historical Society in my hometown. They will sell them to finance their projects and activities.

3. Historians organize panels on "the first west," meaning places such as Kentucky, Tennessee, Illinois, Indiana, Ohio, and western Pennsylvania. Cincinnati is nicknamed the Queen City of the West because of its early-nineteenth-century prominence, and the 1890s-vintage University of Michigan fight song praises "the champions of the West," a reference to the old Western Conference.

Works Cited

Brown, Clara A. Crocker, and Ronald R. Stockton. *Horse Prairie Cemetery, Sesser, Illinois: Tombstone Inscriptions and Family Records.* 2004. Available from the Genealogy Society of Southern Illinois, <http://www.rootsweb.com/~ilgssi/counties.html>.

Cayton, Andrew R. I. *Frontier Indiana.* Bloomington: Indiana UP, 1996.

Degler, Carl N. *At Odds: Women and the Family in America from the Revolution to the Present.* New York: Oxford UP, 1980.

Stockton, Ronald R. "Death on the Frontier: Mortality Patterns in Horse Prairie Cemetery, Franklin County, Illinois, 1840–2002." *Journal of the Illinois State Historical Society* 92.2 (Summer 2003): 146–60.

7

In a Treeless Landscape
A Research Narrative

Kathleen Wider

Because I am a philosopher by trade and training, most of my research begins in my head, first with an intuition and then with the development of rudimentary arguments to support that intuition. My reading of scholarly books and journal articles related to the issue I'm addressing follows these initial steps. Finally, I land back in my head using these sources as support or as counterarguments to whatever position I'm defending. It's a closed circle from head to printed word to head and back to the printed page. This style of research suits me, as it is similar both to finding the puzzle pieces and figuring out how they go together, all this done in the abstract. Great intellectual exercise, and I love it!

However, when my non-philosopher friends and relatives who bought my 1997 book *The Bodily Nature of Consciousness* complained that they could not understand a word of it, I decided that (even though their complaints were at least slightly overstated!) I did need to respond to them. I wanted to write a book that would be both philosophical and literary, one that would reach a broad, general audience. That is when I began a very different kind of research project. Since early in my philosophical career, I had been thinking about the nature of the self, the relationship of the self to the body and to the world, including other people, and the question of self-identity through time. Although I have a graduate degree in English, all my publications were in philosophy and addressed to a small, scholarly audience. That fact didn't extinguish my growing desire to try my hand at literary writing. I didn't have any luck with this when I threw a bit of it into my philosophical essays; the editors or reviewers almost always nixed it. So, given my training, my long-standing intentions, and the complaints, this seemed the moment of truth. I would bring my two areas of interest into equal partnership.

I would explore the philosophical issues about the self that have always intrigued me, but this time I would do so within the context of a specific life, grounding my ideas and discoveries in the concrete details of that life. I chose the life of my paternal grandmother, Augusta Mercedes Maguire Wider, both because it spanned a century and because it was an interesting life. She was part of a homesteading family that moved from a farm in Illinois to Dakota Territory to homestead. In 1882, her parents, Francis and Maggie Maguire, moved their family of two boys and five girls to a 360-acre homestead, nine miles northeast of Plankinton, in what would become the state of South Dakota seven years after their arrival. When Augusta was a teenager, the family left the farm and moved to the small city of Mitchell, forty miles east of Plankinton. She lived there until her death.

From that small prairie town, Augusta created for herself a career as a speaker on the national lecture circuit. She lectured at teachers' institutes, women's clubs, and high school graduations. In small rural schoolhouses and in large university lecture halls, Augusta was at ease. She loved an audience, and the relationship was mutual. The subject of most of her talks was art and beauty and their relationship to the development of a person as an individual and as a citizen. When she died, she left behind several notebooks with outlines of her speeches, lists of hundreds of poems she knew by heart, and brochures she had developed as promotional material to secure speaking engagements across the country. The most important record she left for me to explore was a scrapbook filled with program notes, articles from newspapers reviewing her speeches, and, scattered throughout it, bits and pieces of her family's life. My father had given this scrapbook to his mother when she was in her fifties, and she had noted in it that it should be returned to him after she died. That is how I first came into contact with it. The scrapbook was seductive, drawing me into a world of the past that each page brought alive again. Hearing about my interest in Augusta's life, my aunt Virginia sent me the rest of the material related to her mother's career. So I had found a fascinating life lived through times of radical change in America, including its transformation from a rural to an urban society. I had found a life well documented, with plenty of primary sources to study. I was off and running, although I didn't realize until much later how literal the motion would be.

In 1998, I began this project as many researchers do now: with the Internet. I wanted to find the land my great-grandparents had homesteaded. Augusta's only surviving child, my aunt Virginia, who had actually visited the farm several times as a child, could only remember that the land was west of Mitchell. So I typed into the search window "Aurora County," the name of the county just west of the one Mitchell is in. To my surprise, a list of all the county's original homesteaders appeared on the screen. I remember my excitement as I scanned the list and halfway down found my great-grandfather's name: Francis Maguire. I never suspected at that moment how close I would become, over the next several years, to Francis and Maggie Maguire and their eight children.

As a philosopher, I had spent a great deal of my time among the dead: Plato, Descartes, Kant, Marx, and so on. My relationship to the Maguires, many of whom had died before I was born, was to be as intense and life-changing as my relation to the philosophers I studied. That initial journey into virtual reality taken via the Internet set me off on another journey that took several years and resulted in a style of research and writing far different from any I had used before.

I came to realize quite soon that to fully understand Augusta's life, I would need to know the social and political history within which her life was embedded. I began with the Great Dakota Boom of the 1880s, during which hundreds of thousands came to homestead on the treeless prairie. To understand this mass migration to the plains that had swept my ancestors from the fertile and rolling land of northwest Illinois to the dry, flat landscape of Dakota Territory, I had to research a variety of topics, from the people, animals, and plants that the settlers displaced or destroyed to the reasons for 80 percent of them abandoning their land within twenty years. Many families simply walked away, leaving the barren land that year after year had been stripped of crops and soil by long periods of drought, wind and dust storms, locust invasions, and prairie fires. Driving across the Dakotas, one can still see these farm buildings, standing empty and unused for over a hundred years. I needed to become familiar as well with the congressional debates, which lasted from the 1780s until the 1880s, over what to do with the public lands, whether to sell them to the highest bidder or give them, for a minimal fee, to individual citizens to homestead. This investigation led me to study the impact of the 1803 Louisiana Purchase, which, in doubling the size of the country, added millions of acres to the public domain, out of which were carved all or part of thirteen states, the Dakotas among them. In addition, I needed to acquaint myself with the Lewis and Clark expedition, whose purpose was to map that land. This research led me to sources describing the decision about how to survey this land so it could be offered for a modest fee to new settlers. From the beginning, the government wanted a method of surveying that was objective and permanent, one that would conform to the ideal figures of geometry rather than to the constantly changing shapes of the earth. So they chose the rectangular survey, which described land in numerical terms. A journal entry from my first research trip to South Dakota reflects my experience of this historical fact.

March 2, 2001

Flying over the midsection of the country, with a snow cover below light as air, the earth appears to have been cut to pieces by the roads that follow the section lines of the rectangular survey. In reality, however, the marks are but scorings on the land whose depth is beyond reach. I hadn't realized before that those neat and orderly lines I could see from the sky were the imprint of ideas upon the earth.

The historical research, although it wasn't the kind of research I usually engaged in, was still conventional academic research. But I wanted more than just knowledge of the facts of the history that surrounded my grandmother's family as they came to cultivate the Dakota land. So I set out for South Dakota to experience firsthand the land and its people. After a morning searching through the Aurora County land records, I found the legal description of the homestead and located it on a county map. I was more than ready to experience the land itself. Walking on what had once been the Maguire home farm, I felt at peace, as if I had come home. I was moving closer to the Maguires. In writing this book, at times I felt as though people long gone surrounded me, as alive as those with whom I lived and worked. Not only would I search for the details of Augusta's life and its historical context, I would also need to use my imagination, fueled by sense experience, to dwell within that life. Only then would I be able to offer even partial answers to my philosophical questions. I thought of Kierkegaard's insight, "Life can only be understood backwards, but it must be lived forwards." I would need to look at a life already closed to see if I could discover its significance and in doing so understand something about the significance and the construction of a self-identity for any human life. This project cut closer to the bone than any other ever had. I had to go far beyond an abstract and logical analysis of the questions and their possible answers. I had to go out into the world and deep into myself.

Early evening, July 1998

I am standing on a section line, a gravel road, that in the 1880s divided the Maguire homestead from that of their nearest neighbor. Behind me is a homestead house in ruins. It is gray and sagging. A foreigner to the rural plains, it looks as beautiful to me as any Roman ruin. In front of me are acres of pasture land. As I stand there, the cows in the far distance begin to turn toward me and moo loudly. I'm the one they think has come to give them an early dinner. I imagine that it is this scene, with the sun setting in an open Dakota sky across the flat land of the prairie, with animals hungry for dinner and with the day's work almost behind them, that Francis and Maggie and their children looked out upon over a hundred years earlier.

So began years of varied research, including trips to South Dakota and Elizabeth, Illinois, a town near Augusta's birthplace. I searched land records, haunted cemeteries, dug through the state archives, and met people with various connections to Augusta and the Maguire family. One such encounter was with the present owner of the Maguire homestead land, James Fraser, grandson of the man who homesteaded across from my great-grandparents. He could tell me stories his grandfather had told him about the Maguires: how they lost their cattle herd on the back forty during the blizzard of 1888; how Francis, a man with a wild Irish temper and a love of politics, engaged in heated conversation with whoever came along. He remembered meeting Augusta when he was a teenager and she came to collect the rent for the land his family later bought. She was always the center of attention, he said, as she recounted stories of her latest travels. How much is contained within the span of memory, I thought. In a way, Augusta, Francis, and the other Maguires lived inside the minds of so many people.

Reviewing the hundreds of items in Augusta's scrapbook gave me that same sense of the continuation of a life into others' lives. I read descriptions of her speeches by local news reporters, letters from members of her audiences, programs of the events at which she spoke. I was handling paper she had handled, valuing the same items she had valued, even chronicling her career just as she had done. I came to know her, to a large degree, by examining what she had saved from her lecturing career of more than fifty years.

That fit with my memory of my last visit with Augusta, when she was ninety years old and in a nursing home, in and out of touch with reality. Although I had to tell her repeatedly who I was and who her own children were, she could tell me that she had been a famous lecturer in her day and had traveled widely. She had lost so much by this point, but she had not lost her hold on the career through which she largely formed her identity. To the end of her life a decade later, she could recite an entire poem from memory if given the first line. I'm sure she did it with the same melodious voice I remember when, as a child, I had listened to Augusta reciting poetry to my mother's bridge friends. She was a performance artist, and her voice was her instrument.

I went through her scrapbook numerous times to determine the locations, the dates, and the content of her speeches in order to get some sense of this career and how it co-existed with her life as a mother of four children. When her first three children were small, she confined her lecture career to local venues, often walking to where she would speak, with her two oldest pulling the small wagon that carried the reproductions of artworks she discussed in her lectures. Later, when the oldest boys went off to college, she began to give lectures far from home. She was fortunate in having a husband who was willing to take over for her in her absence. He was a storekeeper, and since the store was right next to their home, he could keep an eye on the two younger children. He'd bring a steak home from the store and cook that for his dinner.

He would give groceries to those too poor to pay cash for them in exchange for their doing the family's laundry. Her daughter, although still in grade school when Augusta's career broadened beyond South Dakota, took care of her younger brother much of the time.

There were days when I would spend hours examining the material in the scrapbook. By evening, my study floor would be littered with bits of yellowed paper, and I would return to the present as though waking from a dream. I came to realize I was a spectator of her life, although not an objective, disinterested, or even innocent one. My narration of her life would be as biased and subjective as her own narration in her scrapbook and letters. How could it be otherwise? I had spent enough years attempting to understand the nature of selfhood in strictly logical terms. This time, however, I got my hands dirty from the labor of detection and in occupying the seat of judgment.

Ultimately I learned, through the perusal of so many rich and diverse research sources, that to understand a life, one must understand the social and political context within which it's lived, the familial history of the person as far backward and forward as possible, the dreams and accomplishments of the person, the other lives that connected and supported the life examined, and so much more. Every thread I pulled from her life led me to another and another. This was the case, for example, when I tried to come to terms with a political speech Augusta had given early in her career. In it, she argued for eugenics, advocating the sterilization of the "unfit" and their (nonvoluntary) placement on "pleasant" farms (a euphemism for prison-like farms). I was appalled. Grandma, I thought, how could you? However, after exploring the history of eugenics in the United States and abroad at the turn of the last century, I understood that her position was inseparable from the ideas of her time. What was important was to understand how she and others, including Theodore Roosevelt and Winston Churchill, could have held such views. This made me realize again how much knowledge is necessary to see the object at which one is looking. Although the topic of this speech was far different from the majority of her speeches, which were on art and education, as her granddaughter I wanted to hide it from public view. I came to accept, however, that to reach even a semblance of understanding of a life, I had to acknowledge both its light and dark dimensions.

Making sense of a person's life is always a work in progress, since each life is embedded within the complex web of connections that constitutes reality. To come to a complete understanding of any one life requires understanding the entire complex. Since it is impossible for humans to attain such understanding, we must settle for a partial and ongoing modification of our understanding. In reflecting on the story of Augusta's life, as told by herself and many others, I understood selfhood in ways that had eluded me when I approached it in the purely analytic mode of philosophy. This doesn't mean that I thought any less of the philosophical approach but that I saw the advantage of blending the lessons learned from the philosophers with the details of Augusta's life as she lived it and as I imagined it. It was this approach that led me to see that there are no final answers to the questions with which I began: What is the significance of any one human life? Out of what do people construct their identity and very personhood? How do time and place contribute to this self-identity? The fact that my understanding of Augusta's life or my own will never be complete frustrates me, but it is also a source of comfort to know that one belongs to more than oneself even in one's own self-identity and beyond the confines of one's lifespan. We are alone neither here nor in the grave.

8

My Grandfather's Trunk

Barry Rohan

His name was Barry Conners. He was an actor who wrote half a dozen plays that ran on Broadway in its golden era, the 1920s. His words launched the Broadway acting careers of Shirley Booth and Humphrey Bogart. He invented the role of a madcap heroine that Marion Davies catapulted to fame in a movie that eighty years later is still shown on Turner Classic Movies. He was among the first playwrights to successfully make the jump from Broadway to the talking movies during the Great Depression. He wrote scripts for the likes of Will Rogers, Spencer Tracy, and Ginger Rogers and helped to put Charlie Chan on the road to success in film.

Yet nothing he wrote for the stage or screen equaled the drama of his own life. In his earliest career as an actor, he was a nationally prominent activist in a pioneer actors' union called the "White Rats" ("Star" spelled backwards). In that real-life role, he staged one of the great comebacks in show business history. After he was blacklisted as an actor following a failed strike, he supported himself for five years as a freelance writer and wilderness guide. Eventually, he emerged in triumph from the woods, becoming a red-hot playwright who at his peak staged three plays on Broadway in a single year, 1925.

Conners also was my maternal grandfather. The fact I know best about him is that he died an untimely death, in 1933, at the age of fifty, three years before I was born. Other than my mother's scattered recollections and a few pictures, I knew little about his life and career.

Then an old theatrical trunk emerged one day and became a passion that took over my life for months. Over that time, I experienced the unique pleasures of research: the joy of discovery, the ability to restore a missing piece of history and to resurrect a life all-but-dead to living memory. The trunk, which I came to think of almost as a living thing, came into my life as an astonishing surprise.

My elderly mother, Renee, was making a bad recovery from a major operation in a hospital in Appleton, Wisconsin. As she lay in what might have been her deathbed, she mentioned her father's theatrical trunk for the first time. This was a trunk my mother had inherited when she was twenty. Somehow she had managed to move it, along with our other possessions, through several apartments and houses in which she raised her four children. Nobody noticed.

The trunk was in a corner of the dimly lighted basement of her apartment building. She said, "You'll need a flashlight to find it. It has his papers."

"His papers?" I was amazed.

"I went through it all at the time of his death," she said. "Afterwards, nobody seemed all that interested."

How could I have missed it all those years? Even in the dim yellow light of the basement of my mother's apartment building, the huge black trunk quickly emerged as one of the largest objects in the room. It was unlocked. I lifted the heavy lid, played a flashlight around the dark insides, and felt my way to the bottom. The trunk was filled with papers; they lay there from corner to corner, over a foot deep, reverently layered.

On top, a book of newspaper clippings, then a huge ledger of neatly scripted notes—apparently bits of business for vaudeville acts. At the bottom, thick, folded manuscripts, dozens of them. I couldn't resist a quick look.

As copies of the turn-of-the-century theater playbills fell under the flashlight, I made the first of many discoveries: my grandfather had experimented with his name. In the earliest playbill, he is "William F. Conners," his real name (which, I later learned, even my mother didn't know). In later playbills, he appears as "Billy Conners" and then "Barry Conners." Was "William F." too formal, "Billy" too undignified?

As I headed to the brighter light upstairs with an armload of paper, I had an insight: "Maybe his whole life is here?"

Then something more disturbing.

"Lord, my mother has given me a stage name!"

And so I was hooked. From that moment, the contents of the trunk belonged to me, and in a strange way, I belonged to the trunk. Now I was responsible for preserving the contents . . . but how? Easy enough to save it from a landlord, but an old trunk filled with paper—one day someone certainly would throw it out.

Right then I decided to read to the bottom of the pile and try to make a story out of what I found. Those scattered pieces of paper would then have new coherence and new dignity as "supporting documents." Who's going to discard supporting documents?

In the weeks that followed, my mother staved off death, which she had irreverently taken to calling The Iceman. As she recovered, she added what information she could about the papers retrieved from the basement. She led me to a dozen letters and other documents from her father that she had stashed away in old books around her apartment and also had mentioned to nobody.

I read histories of vaudeville and the New York theater. I made sorties into everybody's twenty-first-century trunk, the Internet, where I found reviews and copyright information about Grandpa Conners's best-known play, *The Patsy*. A trip to the National Archives in Washington turned up a complete list of his plays on Broadway and, even better, how long they had run, which is more difficult to learn. Someone thoughtfully recorded his movie credits at Twentieth Century Fox. Otherwise, it was pretty lean pickings. Ultimately, it was the trunk and its photos, news clips, and manuscripts saved apparently at random that offered the fuller picture of my grandfather's life.

As I explored Conners's public life, to my surprise a private story-within-the-story began to emerge, an unusual father-daughter love story. I discovered the long-distance bond between my mother and her father and why it had become so important to them both in the last ten years of his life. Both seemed to seek the normal family life that had eluded them. My mother grew up as a child of divorce, yearning for her parents. My grandfather lived most of his adult life on the road in hotel rooms. In a strange way, their bond was commemorated in my grandfather's home-away-from-home, the theatrical trunk that the two of them had forwarded to new addresses for about a hundred years.

Talk about a family tradition.

William F. (Barry) Conners was born in April 1882 in Oil City, Pennsylvania, the son of a country doctor. According to family lore, he earned a law degree but quickly got bored with legal work and joined the theater as an actor. About two dozen of Conners's old playbills show up in the trunk. All seem to have been saved at random, from 1907 to 1913, when a seat at the theater in the smaller cities sold from fifteen to fifty cents, a pair of women's gloves went for a dollar, and a man could buy a bowler hat for two dollars.

He played about everything: romantic leads and stable boys, a farmer, a factory worker, an army officer. He also did standup comedy between the acts. A news clip emerged from much later on, a 1926 interview with the *Christian Science Monitor*, after he had been successful as a Broadway playwright. In it, I heard him speak for the first time other than through my mother as he discusses his acting career. "I was some 15 or 16 years 'trouping' in second- and third-class companies," he told the interviewer. "Never a member of a first-class company such as you have here in New York. The companies I was with were of the 'wildcat' or 'fly-by-night' variety."

My grandfather met my grandmother, Ruby Blackburn, an actress, when both were members of such a theatrical group touring the South. A newspaper clipping—no city indicated—describes the couple's marriage onstage in 1911 after the closing performance. The couple continued to travel the theatrical circuit, and on June 7, 1912, a blazing hot day, my mother, Renee, was born in a hotel room in Fort Smith, Arkansas, where her parents had arrived for a one-night show. It was a difficult birth. For a time, the doctor summoned to the hotel was concerned that Ruby and the baby, weakened by a long labor, might die. Mother and daughter eventually recovered. After leaving the new baby daughter with Ruby's parents in Milwaukee, the couple continued their careers on the road.

The marriage lasted about four years. Ruby apparently had not married Barry for better or worse venues. After she ascended to better roles in bigger cities, their careers diverged, and they parted. You could see this in the playbills. Hers were printed on glossy paper and had venues in Chicago, Detroit, and other big cities. His were published on pulp paper. He got his gigs in places like Waco, Texas, and Duluth, Minnesota.

Actually, his career had taken a disastrous turn. In the years before World War I, Conners traveled the country as a popular speaker in support of a fledgling actors' union, the White Rats. In December 1916, some members staged a spontaneous strike in Oklahoma City that quickly spread to Boston and New York and then nationally. The strike lasted for two months. In the end, the Rats were beaten, their union emasculated.

Besides notices of his union speaking appearances, the trunk contained blank union contracts, a long poem he wrote lamenting the failed strike, and a personal letter of condolence from Harry Mountford, who headed the union. During a subsequent Federal Trade Commission investigation of the theater owners' tactics during the strike, a theater attorney claimed that only a dozen people were blacklisted afterward. Whatever the number, my grandfather was one of them.

By the summer of 1917, Conners had hit rock bottom. At the age of thirty-five, he was banned from making a living in the job to which he had devoted most of his adult life. After failing to find new work, he left for the West Coast. Conners ended up living in a rooming house in the northern California wilderness near Central City. He was able to scratch out a living there for five years by writing vaudeville routines for his old friends and working as a hunting and fishing guide. Some of his writings, including a long, humorous account of a wilderness camping trip, were in the trunk.

My interviews with my mother led to an important paper carefully folded away in another of her old books. It documented an unusual legal agreement with Edward Esmonde, a New York theatrical agent and longtime friend of my grandfather's. In return for half of Conners's income from his creative work,

Esmonde agreed to establish him in an apartment in New York City and pay all expenses while he wrote plays.

And so Conners left the California wilderness behind. After a joyous reunion with his eleven-year-old daughter, still living with her maternal grandparents in Milwaukee, he went on to New York. He set up shop in an apartment building overlooking 58th Street, near Central Park, where Esmonde lived with his wife and daughter, and began working on several plays.

Shortly thereafter, he fired off a letter to daughter Renee in which he could hardly contain his excitement: "On Monday I have a conference with the two men who are going to do the play [*Mad Honeymoon*]. I saw them yesterday and they were both wonderful to me—told me how delighted they were with the play. . . . And on top of that they talked of doing some of the other plays."

Renee sent a return letter in which she shyly asked for advice about which picture of him she ought to wear in the gold locket he had given her. It was the first exchange in a long correspondence between the two as Barry moved to reinforce the new relationship and reestablish himself as a real father. From August 1922 through the summer of 1923, Conners wrote her regularly chatty and affectionate letters, which my mother carefully saved. He sent pictures and playbills, reports on the status of his plays, and offered tourist-like impressions of New York. The letters also slowly assumed the burden of repairing a growing rift between Renee and her absent mother. Actress Ruby, also working in New York, was rarely home. Worse, she didn't write and returned some of her daughter's letters with punctuation and spelling corrected. Renee seemed to have pretty well given up on her.

Over the next eight years, Conners wrote seven comedies produced on Broadway. One of these was *Hell's Bells*, in which Shirley Booth and Humphrey Bogart made their Broadway debuts as young lovers. Both their careers got a boost from the critics. An undated and unidentified review in the trunk noted simply, "Miss Booth is charming and handles her proposal scene beautifully. Mr. Bogart was the best actor in the company."

My grandfather saved scores of reviews of his plays but neglected to date many of them or, sometimes, even to note the name of the newspaper. As time went on, he got ever more careless about that. He also saved various drafts of *The Patsy*, his most enduring play. After its nine-month run on Broadway, in 1925–26, it lived on for many years in new amateur and professional productions. (There are references in the trunk to productions in London, Prague, and Budapest.)

The play still has legs. A movie version of the play, starring Marion Davies, has been shown several times in recent years. A new, glowing review of the refurbished movie is also on-line. The story, characters, and much of the language of the original play are captured in the movie.

The strength of the play is a romantic leading lady who is not merely beautiful but also clever, sassy, and unpredictable. Many critics fell in love with the character Patricia Harrington and thought she was a new and refreshing heroine on the American stage. The part substantially boosted the careers of three actresses who played the role in the 1920s. The play is a twist on Cinderella. Patricia, a mischievous flapper, is the underdog pitted against her older sister, Grace, and her socially ambitious mother. Patricia is always in her mother's doghouse. Patricia finds a staunch ally in her father, Bill, with whom she has a warm relationship. But Bill travels a lot on business, and so he fails to save Patricia and straighten out his shrewish wife until late in the play.

The striking thing about *The Patsy* is how closely the character of the mother mimics Conners's ex-wife, Ruby, who seemed born to play the part of a woman whose ambition has made her a neglectful, even nasty, mother. Like Patricia Harrington, Renee felt ignored and needed to be emotionally rescued by her loving father. Even as his play was running on Broadway, Conners did his best to achieve that. (But he, too, was hampered by the need to be almost always out of town on business.) Some of the play's dialogue between father and daughter treads the edge of actual words spoken to Renee by her mother and father on a number of occasions. As in real life, Patsy's father tries to reassure his disbelieving daughter that her mother really loves her, all evidence to the contrary. And he blames her mother's inability to show her love on the trauma of Patricia's birth.

Alas, life is not fiction; unlike Patsy's father, my grandfather was never able to straighten out Ruby. Even in the play, mother and daughter are never exactly reconciled. In real life, Conners celebrated his newfound success by inviting Renee and her grandmother Blackburn to join him for summers in the New York area. He also began providing substantial support to the Blackburn family. This eventually included a princess-like $100-a-month allowance for Renee (the equivalent of over $1,000 in today's currency). By 1925, he moved out of his New York hotel and into the first permanent home of his adult life, an old farmhouse in the growing artist colony near Westport, Connecticut.

Beginning in 1926, fourteen-year-old Renee, chaperoned by her grandmother, began spending her summers in Connecticut with her father. The ritual continued throughout her teenage years and later included trips to Hollywood. Conners's very own Patricia Harrington had been rescued in style.

After the stock market crash in 1929 and the onset of the Depression, New York theater audiences and money for new productions began to dry up. Conners joined Fox Film Corporation as a screenwriter in 1930. (The company would become Twentieth Century Fox in a corporate merger five years later.) Over the next two and a half years, Conners wrote or co-wrote the scripts for sixteen movies, including comedies, dramas, mysteries, and westerns. Some were original, some adapted from novels. Among the adaptations were three of the earliest Charlie Chan movies. The trunk shed no light on this part of his career, but I found a full list of his screenwriting credits on the Internet Movie Database Web site (imdb.com).

The record comes to an abrupt end on January 4, 1933, in an event marked by the shortest article in the trunk's collection that had so long served as the family's only obituary. A two-inch-column story in a Los Angeles newspaper notes simply that Barry Conners, Fox Film Corp. screenwriter, died of suffocation in a fire in his Hollywood apartment building. But now, thanks to the possibilities of research, the old news clipping has new power. My grandfather's memory has been more fully restored to the family, and the emotional landscape has changed. For the first time, I feel the impact of his death and the tragedy of such a promising life cut short. I not only know him better but also better understand a crucial father-daughter relationship in my mother's emotional life, which, to my astonishment, has played on Broadway and late-night TV.

Finally, the project provided the satisfaction of justice achieved. A once-neglected story is now available in perpetuity on the public record. The research produced a 10,000-word biography, and it and several boxes of Conners's personal papers have been accepted into the University of Wisconsin's collection of theatrical history. Meanwhile, my mother's quiet obsession—the trunk—has moved on, this time to my home in suburban Detroit.

An unusual family tradition continues.

Works Consulted

Guernsey, Otis L. *Directory of the American Theater, 1894–1971.* New York: Dodd, Mead, 1971.

Internet Movie Database, <http://us.imdb.com>.

Laurie, Joe. *Vaudeville: From the Honky-Tonks to the Place.* New York: Henry Holt, 1953.

Leither, Samuel L. *The Encyclopedia of the New York Stage, 1920–1930.* Vols. 1 and 2. New York: Greenwood, 1985.

Lukas, Anthony J. *Big Trouble: A Murder in a Small Western Town Sets Off a Struggle for the Soul of America.* New York: Simon and Schuster, 1997.

Maltin, Leonard. *Movie and Video Guide, 2000 Edition.* New York: Signet, 1999.

Mantle, Burns, ed. *Best Plays of 1923–24.* New York: Dodd, Mead, 1976.

———. *Best Plays of 1924–25*. New York: Dodd, Mead, 1976.

———. *Best Plays of 1925–1926*. New York: Dodd, Mead, 1976.

———. *Best Plays of 1928–29*. New York: Dodd, Mead, 1976.

Robertson, David. *The History of World Cinema*. New York: Stein and Day, 1973.

Rusie, Robert. "Broadway 101: The History of the Great White Way." *Talkin' Broadway*. 1999. <http://www.talkinbroadway.com/bway101/5.html>.

Slide, Anthony. *The Encyclopedia of Vaudeville*. Westport, CT: Greenwood, 1994.

Snyder, Robert W. *Voice of the City: Vaudeville and Popular Culture in New York*. New York: Oxford UP, 1989.

Stein, Charles, ed. *American Vaudeville as Seen by Its Contemporaries*. New York: Knopf, 1984.

In Search of Rememory

But I had to know. This might be the postcolonial era, but here remains the colony, no matter the convolutions and euphemisms. And here remains this man, this man who had a revolutionary force and no revolution, things I knew nothing about apart from my father's nostalgia about the man of *el Yunque, mi tía*'s boyfriend. And here were the politics of my father when I was a child—my father, who seemed to give up talking of politics, to give up the idea that he would return to the Island, that the Island was there to return to, the permanence of exile, albeit an exile to a wife who did not desire a return to the homeland where her memories are of abandonment and being sold as chattel, an exile in the estrangement of his children from his culture. And Dad would introduce me as "my son, Fidel," a matter I took as ridicule when I was twenty-five and when I was fifty came to wonder if it were intended to be honorific. And memories of Dad: "Straight ahead, and get Castro!," laughing at the obsession against Castro and its failure (Castro having now survived nine hostile U.S. presidents).

Exile. Alienation. What does one do when one becomes fully conscious of the alienation that arises from exile, of being racialized, of knowing something ain't right and there ain't no puttin' it right but can't be no ignoring the wrong? Racism, its tie to colonialism, its tie to language and language-in-action, its corrosive effect, it's leaving holes in memory, like empty pockets in the brain. Dad's son had made it, a professor with minor notoriety, the middle class now, speaking and writing against racism, trying to understand what allows racism to continue when biological explanations fall apart, when stereotypes are stereotypically realized to be mere stereotypes, the son who looks at language, thinking nothing happens without the word, the son who nevertheless has to feel the irony of making a prideful claim—I am a Puerto Rican—spoken calmly, a simple assertion, a matter of fact, yet realizing that this is a Puerto Rican who knows nothing beyond Dad's stories of Puerto Rico, a Nuyorican, but one whose time in New York preceded the word, the identity, "Nuyorican." Exile and Alienation: like amnesia, lost memory. It was time to recover the culture, its past, its connection to who my father was and who our people were.

Serendipity

Research is a funny process. So much of it is serendipity. A student having to take a Spanish translation exam hands me the piece she's submitting for the translation. Its title is "Hostos, Martí y Albizu: *Su Critica del Imperialismo*." Haltingly, I learn of Albizu, of his words, of his anti-imperialist discourse.

I look to archives in English. I find some biographies. A friend and contributor to this volume, Gail Okawa, has been to the National Archives in

Part Three

When Personal, Cultural, and Historical Memory Shape the Politics of the Archives

9

Colonial Memory, Colonial Researcl
A Preamble to a Case Study

Victor Villanueva

The interpretation of our reality through patterns not our ow
only to make us ever more unknown, ever less free, ever mor
—Gabriel Ga

A Memory (2003)

His deathbed was an industrial hospital bed in a cold, ascetic
room in the hospice wing of the giant VA hospital in Spokane,
ton. The thick, wavy black hair that he once had been so prou
gone, some white wisps left, yet a fine-toothed comb still reste
He had been in a coma. His wife, his children, his grandchild
words of love to him, prayers to wing him along. A cough, a cl
teeth, and a tightening of muscles that pulled him into a fetal
and he was dead. Dad. Dead. So far from home.

This is where the story starts. With Dad.

Dad would speak of the young man who had dated his sister.
man had wavy black hair and a good physique (that mattered
good physique), and the young man loved the Island. The U.S.
ment had finally figured out that the men who walked around
black guayaberas, the loose-fitting shirts of the tropics, were rev
ies, members of the Nationalist Party of Puerto Rico, led by Dr
Albizu Campos, el Maestro, the Teacher.

The young man who had dated Dad's sister, mi tía Margar
run into the tropical rainforest, el Yunque, where Dad, himsel
would bring him dry clothes and food.

I don't know the story beyond that.

Dad would always go on to lament that his sister married so

Washington, D.C. She connects me to her contact there. Preparing to go, I search the Internet. What I find, I find disturbing. Most of it concerns the assassination of John F. Kennedy; a summary of past assassins and assassination attempts is all that can be found on Albizu. But he had never assassinated nor taken part in an assassination. Surely Dad would have mentioned that. I knew of the Puerto Rican attempt on President Truman but had not heard of Albizu's involvement. The language of the FBI reports amounted to pointing to Albizu as the inspiration of assassination. The United States likes, needs, ringleaders. Decide I'll have to take a different tack. That tack has yet to develop fully. This is a preamble, after all.

Another student, a Puerto Rican doctoral student (now a professor) of sociology, hands me a manuscript, *La Palabra Como Delito* (The Word as Crime). And in my less-than-fluent Spanish, I discover that the pictures contained therein were all taken by the FBI in its long surveillance of Albizu. And I discover the basis of all that surveillance, the crimes for which he would spend the majority of his life in prison: speeches. Twelve speeches, in particular, and a law (Law 53 of a general gag order—*la Ley de la Mordaza*) that stipulated that the word was very literally the equivalent of weapons ("Ensayo introductorio" 11). But because I am English dominant, a postcolonial product, I try to find those twelve speeches in English.

But I find only fragments of the speeches of Dr. Albizu Campos in English. This is the case study I would draw, this man called a terrorist, this man sentenced to eighty years' imprisonment for what he said—sedition. My need to recover something of ancestry becomes deeply tied to rhetoric. His is the crime of being an effective rhetor.

Yet how effective was he really? It's hard to see what his danger might have been. He was a hero followed by few. His was the voice heard by the many but truly listened to only by the few, the voice whose rhetoric condemned him, whose rhetoric was a crime. He was called "el Maestro," a powerful speaker, with thousands gathering to listen to his deliberative rhetoric for freedom. He urged the people to reclaim their cultural history and national symbols, like the national anthem and the *monoestrella*, the one-star flag. But though he spoke for the worker and the peasant, his appeal was limited to the middle class when time came for votes. For all his speaking, for all his attracting of audiences, ballots told of a remarkably small following.

Research now takes a traditional turn. Books. Discover the history of Puerto Rico. Find what I can on Albizu. Eventually, thanks to the Internet, I find the one book written in English that is about Albizu. It dates to 1971. One must wonder how that can be. From here, I follow the trail. It's still ahead. But this much I know:

Albizu's Context

Pedro Albizu Campos was—is—seen as a revolutionary. But there was no revolution; there will be no revolution. Revolution requires unity. Unity means a clear understanding of one's status. But Puerto Rico's status, its identity, is a discursive whirlwind. A rhetorician reels at the obfuscation. Puerto Rico is a free nation: that's the Spanish rendering of a "commonwealth." It is a commonwealth, free, except that it's a protectorate, under the protection of the U.S. state and military, the military that until recently used an inhabited island of Puerto Rico for target practice with fully armed heavy weaponry. So Puerto Rico has a colonial relationship to the United States, with neocolonial economic dependence on the United States. Its people cannot vote for the president of the United States, can't have a president of its own, and can only provide a non-voting representative to the U.S. Congress. Puerto Rico is a free, autonomous, dependent, protected, neocolonial, colonial state with postcolonial identity problems. Albizu would have been seven years old when the United States first bombed Puerto Rico during the Spanish-American War.

The United States took Manifest Destiny to a new plane in 1898, at the end of a century of revolutions throughout the world, including the U.S. South rebelling against its North. At the same time as the U.S. Civil War, Spain was dealing with a number of revolutions from her subject nations. By the 1860s, Spain had acquiesced; the spirit of Simón Bolívar had remained strong. By 1897, Puerto Rico had created its own economic infrastructure. It believed Spain was about to set it free.

Then, while Puerto Rico seemed to be winning the war of diplomacy with Spain, the revolution in Cuba seemed more and more likely to end with a black Cuban victory. The wealthy white Cubans would have none of it. And the United States, still reeling from the Haitian revolution, would have none of it. An American ship is mysteriously blown up, the *Maine*. Spaniards are blamed. Or was it the Cubans? In a famous story, it is said that when correspondent Frederick Remington wrote William Randolph Hearst to ask to come back home from a peaceful Cuba in 1898, Hearst wrote back: "Please remain. You furnish the pictures and I'll furnish the war." And war it was. And the United States wins the Philippines, Guam, Cuba, and Puerto Rico (Creelman 177–78).

> FROM SANDRA MARÍA ESTEVES:
> IT IS RAINING TODAY
>
> . . .
> La lluvia contains our history
> In the space of each tear Cicique valleys and hills

Taíno, Arawak, Carib, Ife, Congo, Angola, Mesa
Mandinko, Dahome, Amer, African priests tribes
Of the past
Murdered ancestors
Today, voices in the mist
Where is our history?
What are the names washed down the sewer
In the septic flood?
I pray to the rain
Give me back my rituals
Give back truth
Return the remnants of my identity. . . .
Speak to me of rain.

Albizu's Beginnings

Dr. Pedro Albizu Campos was born in Tenerías Village of Ponce in Puerto Rico. He had been born to Juana Campos and Alejandro Albizu. Doña Juana's brother was Juan Morel Campos, a famous Puerto Rican composer of *danzas*, the classical music of Puerto Rico. Don Pedro was born of the Island and its culture.

In 1912, Pedro Albizu Campos is awarded a scholarship to study chemistry at the University of Vermont. A year later he enters Harvard, where he earns a law degree. While at Harvard, he studies law, English literature, philosophy, chemical engineering, and military science. He learns English, French, German, Portuguese, Italian, Latin, and Greek. Then comes the First World War. Albizu enters the U.S. Army, a second lieutenant, assigned to an African American regiment. This is his first sustained exposure to U.S. racism. The United States sees him as black, though given the breadth of racial mixes of Puerto Rico—and all its labels (from *blanco* to *moreno* to *amarillo* to *café-con-leche* to *trigueño* to others I barely remember)—he would have likely been seen as *mulato*. His wife, a Peruvian, thought he was Hindu when they first met (aided in part by that first meeting having taken place during a lecture by the famous Hindu intellectual Rabindranath Tagore). Albizu's exposure to U.S. racism within the military affects his attitudes toward the United States and its relation to what he consistently referred to as the motherland, Puerto Rico.

After the war, Albizu returns to Harvard, where he works with world leaders who are seeking independence for their own countries. He works with the Indian nationalist leader under Gandhi, Sudas Ghandra Gose, and with Rabindranath Tagore. When don Pedro meets Irish statesman Eamon de Valera at Harvard, he helps to draft the constitution for the Irish Free State and takes part in establishing several centers in Boston for Irish independence. In the midst of all of this, he meets the Peruvian scholar and scientist Dr. Laura Meneses. They marry in 1922. Upon obtaining his law degree, Dr. Albizu Campos declines a post on the U.S. Supreme Court and another with the U.S. diplomatic corps, choosing to return to Puerto Rico to take on the causes of the poor and disaffected.

Albizu the Activist

In 1922, Albizu joins the Puerto Rican Unity Party. When, in 1924, the Party joins with the Republican Party and decides not to pursue Puerto Rican independence, Albizu leaves the Unity Party and joins the Nationalist Party of Puerto Rico, where he is quickly elected vice president. Three years later, he travels to Santo Domingo, Haiti, Cuba, Mexico, Panama, Peru, and Venezuela, seeking solidarity for the Puerto Rican independence movement. By 1930, he is elected president of the Nationalist Party and forms the first Women's Nationalist Committee. Julia de Burgos is a member. During his presidency, in 1931, Albizu exposes the conducting of experiments by members of the Rockefeller Institute. He accuses the Rockefeller Institute of deliberately infecting several Puerto Rican citizens with cancer, causing the deaths of thirteen. Dr. Cornelius Rhoades, the chief pathologist for the study, admits to the charge, stating the "Porto Ricans [*sic*] are the dirtiest, laziest, most degenerate and thievish race of men ever to inhabit this sphere," so he had done his "best to further the process of extermination by killing off eight and transplanting cancer into several more. . . . All physicians take delight in the abuse and torture of the unfortunate subjects" (Vankin and Whalen 297). Rhoades was later given a seat on the Atomic Energy Commission and awarded the Legion of Merit by the U.S. government. For all that, the Nationalist Party loses significantly at the following year's election, 1932. In 1933, Albizu represents sugarcane workers against the U.S. sugar interests in Puerto Rico and wins.

Then the trouble.

In 1935, four Nationalists are killed by police under the command of Colonel E. Francis Riggs at the University of Río Piedras. The following year, Nationalists Hiram Rosado and Elias Beauchamp kill Colonel Riggs. They are arrested and executed without a trial. Albizu publicly declares them martyrs and heroes. That declaration is sufficient for the San Juan federal court to order Albizu's arrest for his rhetoric, for sedition. A jury of seven Puerto Ricans and five North Americans vote seven to five not guilty. Judge Robert A. Cooper calls for a new jury, this time with ten North Americans and two Puerto Ricans seated. Albizu is found guilty (ten to two voting guilty). He is sentenced to ten years' imprisonment at a federal penitentiary in the United States. The year is 1937.

Nineteen forty-seven. Albizu returns to Puerto Rico, where, according to the FBI, he is believed to be preparing, along with other members of the Nationalist Party, for an armed struggle against the proposed plans to change Puerto Rico's political status into a commonwealth of the United States. In 1948, the founder of the Popular Democratic Party, José Luis Muñoz Marín, is elected governor of Puerto Rico by a majority of the people. In 1950, the U.S. Congress declares Puerto Rico a commonwealth, along the lines of Massachusetts, Pennsylvania, Virginia, and Kentucky. Yet Puerto Rico is only statelike in its form of government, not in its relation to the other forty-eight United States (Alaska and Hawaii not becoming states until 1959). Within Puerto Rico, "commonwealth" is translated to "Estado Libre Asociado," literally "Free Associated State." Yet it is generally recognized that Puerto Rico's association to the United States is neither as a state nor as free. Recognizing the irony in Puerto Rico's new status, a group of Puerto Rican Nationalists storms Governor Muñoz Marín's mansion, la Fortaleza, on October 30, 1950. As part of a coordinated effort, Nationalists simultaneously attack the U.S. Capitol Building and Blair House, where President Truman is in residence while the White House is under repair. Albizu is charged with masterminding the attacks, or at least inspiring them, Law 53 stating that to advocate overthrow is the same as taking part in overthrow—words as weapons. Albizu is sentenced to eighty years' imprisonment.

Albizu is pardoned in 1953 by Governor Muñoz Marín, but the pardon is revoked the following year, after the 1954 Nationalist attack on the U.S. House of Representatives, when four Puerto Rican Nationalists fired into the gallery of the Capitol Building in Washington, D.C. Some members of Congress are wounded. The shooters do not resist arrest, claiming the action was to attract the world's attention to their cause. The Nationalists claim no association to Albizu.

While in prison, Albizu repeatedly charges that he is a target of human radiation experiments. U.S. officials and the U.S. and Puerto Rican press dismiss the allegations as the ravings of a madman. Yet his skin is severely swollen and cracking. Although Albizu's allegations are never proven, the U.S. Department of Energy does disclose in 1995 that human radiation experimentation had indeed been conducted on prisoners without prisoner consent from the 1950s through the 1970s. By 1964, don Pedro is partially paralyzed from a stroke and is dying. In November of that year, Governor Muñoz Marín again pardons Albizu. The following year, Pedro Albizu Campos dies: April 21, 1965.

Albizu's Politics

Although there is common sentiment that Albizu was a communist, like Cuba's revolutionary leader, Albizu was politically very conservative. Albizu believed that Puerto Rico's cultural ways should remain loyal to the cultural ideals of Spain and that those ideals are best reflected in Roman Catholicism. In other words, Albizu was a Christian Democrat, Latin America's conservative ideology. He was a Christian Democrat who believed that Puerto Rico and its people should be free.

Don Pedro argued in court and at the podium that the U.S. occupation of Puerto Rico had been illegal. He claimed that the Paris Peace Treaty of 1898 should have been nullified by the fact that Spain had previously granted autonomy to Puerto Rico in 1897. Having granted Puerto Rico independence, Spain had no rights with which to hand it to the United States. Further, Puerto Rico had never participated in the treaty, nor had its people been consulted. Puerto Rico's right to freedom, Albizu declared, was no less than the United States' right, fought for through the subversion of the Boston Tea Party and the outright rebellion led by George Washington. Yet unlike Washington against Britain, Albizu had never borne arms against the United States. Albizu was armed only with words, words of weapons: "The motherland's right to independence is not open to discussion. And if it is discussed, it will be with bullets" (qtd. in Ribes Tovar 190). It would be these words and others like them that would cause A. Cecil Snyder, the U.S. district attorney for Puerto Rico from 1933 to 1942, to write to J. Edgar Hoover that Albizu, through the Nationalist Party, "has conducted throughout the Island a campaign of public speeches in favor of Independence which constantly harp on the fact that the purpose of the United States is to exploit Puerto Rico and Its citizens." Albizu had become an irritant who not only claimed exploitation but proved it, thanks to the sugar industry, thanks to the Rockefeller Institute, thanks to the everyday experience of Puerto Ricans generally. Yet for all the ire, he remained a symbolic figure, not one who ever really moved the masses, never rousing more than 5 percent of Puerto Rico's voters.

The Spanish-speaking nations of this hemisphere nevertheless remember him, honor him. Sources in Spanish are plentiful. The twelve speeches that condemned him remain intact, extant, in print—in Spanish. But here I am, a postcolonial subject, an English professor, no revolutionary, needing to understand something of my memory, my cultural memory, my ancestral memory, needing to understand how words that don't incite people to revolution can be seen as dangerously revolutionary.

A year before he died, Dad and Mom were in my living room after at-
tending my oldest daughter's wedding. I played the Buena Vista Social
Club for them; watched them dance that Puerto Rican version of the
mambo, what we called "dirty mambo" when I was a kid, what later
became salsa, Mom and Dad moving hips and rubber knees, the eighty-
year-old man and his seventy-five-year-old sweetie.

I had kindled their memory. And I had kindled my own, of my parents
and how they partied when I was young.

But something else was kindled. I thought of Ry Cooder, this musician
who ventured into Cuba to capture the music of my parents' youth and
in some sense my own. I didn't fret over appropriation. I wondered at
his courage.

Courage.

The research will have to take me to Puerto Rico. But I find that I
am afraid to venture to Puerto Rico, a deep-seated shame in having lost
so much, even though it was not my doing, not my shame, not even my
parents', echoes of Franklin Roosevelt speaking of the Anglicization of the
people of Puerto Rico as a necessary component to Operation Bootstrap.
Teddy to FDR—the Roosevelts—and my ancestry and my status, the
white racialized, proud of my heritage, embarrassed to confront it because
of the postcolonial process of erasure and the substitution of the loss of
memory with myth, the myth that a language, Spanish, is a race.

But Mami and Dad won't dance again in my living room. Nevermore.
And I will have to face the shame. Alone. To keep their memory alive, and
to keep alive the memory of a people.

Works Cited

Acosta, Ivonne. "Ensayo introductorio: La palabra como delito." *La Palabra*
Como Delito: Los discursos por los que condenaron a Pedro Albizu Campos,
1948–1950. San Juan: Editorial Cultural, 1993. 11–24.

Creelman, James. *On the Great Highway: The Wanderings and Adventures of*
a Special Correspondent. Boston: Lothrop, 1901.

"DOE Openness: Human Radiation Experiments." *U.S. Department of Energy.*
May 23, 2006 <http://www.eh.doe.gov/ohre/>.

Esteves, Sandra María, "It Is Raining Today." *Puerto Rican Writers at Home*
in the USA: An Anthology. Ed. Faythe Turner. Seattle: Open Hand, 1991.
188.

García Márquez, Gabriel. "The Solitude of Latin America: Nobel Lecture." *Nobelprize.org.* Dec. 8, 1982. Oct. 29, 2005 <http://nobelprize.org/literature/laureates/1982/marquez-lecture.html>.

Kaplan, Amy. *The Anarchy of Empire in the Making of U.S. Culture.* Cambridge, MA: Harvard UP, 2005.

Laviera, Tato. "Graduation Speech." *Aloud: Voices from the Nuyorican Poets Café.* Ed. Miguel Algarin, Bob Holman, and Nicole Blackman. New York: Owl, 1994. 332.

National Archives. Warren Commission, Appendix 7. *Archives.gov.* May 23, 2006 <archives.gov/research_room/jfk/warren_commission/warren_commission_report_appendix7.html>.

Ribes Tovar, Frederico. *Albizu Campos: Puerto Rican Revolutionary.* New York: Plus Ultra, 1971.

Rojas Osorio, Carlos. "Hostos, Martí y Albizu: Su Critica del Imperialismo." *Exégesis: Revista de la Universidad de Puerto Rico en Humacao* 15 (2002): 55–58.

Snyder, A. Cecil. *Carta al director del FBI Edgar Hoover sobre don Pedro Albizu Campos y el Partido Nacionalista puertorriqueño. Puerto Rico en breve.* May 23, 2006 <http://www.preb.com/FBI /15en1936.htm>.

Vankin, Jonathan, and John Whalen. *The Fifty Greatest Conspiracies of All Time: History's Biggest Mysteries, Coverups, and Cabals.* Sacramento: Citadel, 1994.

Wagenheim, Kal, and Olga Jiménez de Wagenheim, eds. *The Puerto Ricans: A Documentary History.* Princeton: Markus Weiner, 2002.

10

Unbundling
Archival Research and Japanese American Communal Memory of U.S. Justice Department Internment, 1941–45

Gail Y. Okawa

> *"My dear Sumi," he wrote on pale blue paper*
> *stamped "Detained Alien Enemy Mail EXAMINED."*
> *Thirty-five letters, formally signed,*
> *"from your father, Tamasaku Watanabe"*
> *from Lordsburg and Santa Fe, New Mexico,*
> *bundled and tied with a deep red cord.*
> *My mother's letters to him*
> *at Lordsburg Alien Internment Camp and*
> *Santa Fe Detention Station,*
> *kept long past his death,*
> *bundled and tied with care,*
> *stored in old cardboard boxes.*
> *Each page captures time and feeling,*
> *constructs memory for descendants*
> *who care to read them,*
> *memory so fragile that it can be lost*
> *in an oversight,*
> *in a word.*

I was born during a World War II blackout, I've been told. My mother was carried to Queen's Hospital in an ambulance, probably one of the only vehicles allowed on the road under those conditions in Honolulu, even a year after Pearl

---

I dedicate this essay to the memory of my grandfather Reverend Tamasaku Watanabe (1882–1968) and to the memories of Kazumi Matsumoto (1902–2003) and Reverend Shingetsu Akahoshi (1907–2007), internee survivors whom I had the privilege of meeting and interviewing for this study; both lived one hundred years.

Harbor was attacked. As a child, I was shielded completely from the war with the exception of duck-and-cover exercises in preschool and the wailing sirens of ambulances that terrified me for years.

I didn't know that my maternal grandfather, Tamasaku Watanabe, was absent and don't remember exactly when he appeared in my life, a tall, quiet, almost austere man, a Presbyterian minister who was a physical presence once or twice a year when he came to visit us in Honolulu from the Island of Maui. My warmest memory of him comes from sometime in my pre-adolescence: When he was on one of his visits, I had to stay at home from school one day with a cold and made egg salad and Spam sandwiches for our lunch. A man of few words, he expressed his enjoyment and approval of the simple meal by smiling impishly and remarking that I should open a sandwich shop—a compliment that I've never forgotten.

When I was in high school in Honolulu, I first learned from a neighbor that this grandfather had been imprisoned in an American internment camp on the mainland during World War II. My family had never talked about it, and neither did he. I was shaken and ran home to question my parents; I remember them confirming the fact of his incarceration and saying only that "he came back a changed man." It seemed to be a closed subject at that point, and I don't remember pursuing it. He died of cancer in 1968 when I was away from home, teaching in a Virginia women's college.

Many years later, in the 1990s, my mother shared some letters that her father had written to her from addresses in Lordsburg and Santa Fe, New Mexico, mostly on light blue government aerograms printed with the English, German, Italian, and Japanese imperatives "Do not write here! Nicht hier schreiben! Non scrivete qui! Kaku nakare!" and stamped with "Detained Alien Enemy Mail examined by [censor's initials] U.S.I.&N.S."[1] In some cases, "Prisoner of War Mail" had been crossed out and "Internee Mail" written in its place, to me an interesting confusion and conflation of terms and people. In all, there were eight letters from the Lordsburg Internment Camp and twenty-seven from the Santa Fe Detention Station (later called the Santa Fe Alien Internment Camp, according to return addresses). Initially, I thought they would provide some researcher with rich material, hesitating myself due to the historical and private nature of the documents. Yet later, as I opened box after cardboard box and found documents carefully bundled and labeled among my grandfather's papers, I began to feel that he had left them for us—for me—to understand what had happened to him during those war years. This is a story about such bundles, the archival work that brings them back to us, and the process of constructing a community memory—unbundling and re-bundling as processes being as intricate as the bundling itself. Eventually, the rebundling would evolve into a book-length study on the mainland internment of Hawai'i's *issei* (the immigrant generation).

Gaps

Although Tamasaku Watanabe was a diligent and meticulous record keeper—he had pocket-sized notebooks and diaries in his boxes, dating from 1922 through 1967—his notes from December 7, 1941,[2] through the war years to 1944 are mysteriously absent. And although he kept many, if not all, of his important papers (in English and Japanese) from that period, piecing them together has left gaping holes and raised further questions for me. Why was he arrested? What was he charged with? Where was he imprisoned, and by whom? What kind of life did he lead in those facilities that President Franklin D. Roosevelt referred to as "concentration camps"[3] back in 1936? Who were his friends and associates? What kinds of dilemmas did he face, and how did he face them? In this research project, I have sought to fill some of those gaps by locating other pieces of the puzzle.

Now I know that Reverend Watanabe was one of nearly nine hundred Japanese immigrants in Hawai'i who had a fate still relatively unknown to the general American public. One of the less-known facts about the World War II internment is that the U.S. Department of Justice (DOJ), as early as December 7, 1941—and using previously prepared lists—seized and separately imprisoned nearly eight thousand Japanese resident aliens (Kashima 125) from the continent and the then-territories of Hawai'i and Alaska.[4] Like Reverend Watanabe, they were predominantly male immigrants, heads of households, and community leaders detained, in most cases, for reasons no more substantial than that they were Japanese. This little-known story is told over and over again in internment literature and dramatized in films—fathers taken from their families who often heard nothing about them for weeks or months. Although many were longtime residents of the United States, as Japanese immigrants they were designated as "aliens ineligible for citizenship," based on their race by discriminatory naturalization laws in the 1920s, and then labeled "alien enemies" when hostilities broke out between the United States and their country of origin, based on the Alien Enemies Act of 1798. Plans for their imprisonment were premeditated and covert, related to long and complex surveillance operations. Paul Clark relates evidence revealing that some camps were being constructed in New Mexico at Fort Stanton as early as January 1941, followed by Fort Missoula in Montana and Fort Lincoln in North Dakota (8). In all, the Justice Department oversaw thirteen camps with many of the Japanese internees passing through or being incarcerated in Santa Fe over the course of the war.

Gail Y. Okawa

The Road to Santa Fe

In one of the ironies of life, I had been drawn to Santa Fe at least four times earlier—to the Pueblo cultures, the adobe buildings, the museums of Native cultures and international folk art, the stark surrounding landscape of juniper trees and tumble weeds, the Sangre de Cristo mountains. Only on the last two trips, in 1999 and 2000, did I have a vague awareness of my grandfather's presence there decades before. At those times, no one I talked to could tell me where the internment camp had been located; it was as though it had never existed.

In the fall of 2001, I learned that a group called the Committee for the World War II Santa Fe Internment Camp Historical Marker was attempting to raise funds to establish a memorial marker at the Santa Fe Internment Camp site, and I excitedly contacted Colonel Joe Ando, U.S. Air Force (Retired), the son of an internee and the co-chair of the committee. Finding this effort in progress, having the reality of the internment camp confirmed, and learning that there were others who sought to preserve this nearly forgotten part of history, I was inspired to compose a sabbatical leave research proposal on "The Politics of Language and Identity: The Case of Japanese Immigrants in U.S. Justice Department Internment Camps during World War II." A rather ambitious and, I now know, naive proposal due to its broad scope, it set the theoretical stage for me to examine the general Justice Department camp experience through the lenses of language, literacy, and identity among Japanese internees.

In the midst of this, on the morning of September 11, 2001, as I was driving to teach my classes at Youngstown State University, I heard words on National Public Radio that called to mind Orson Welles's "War of the Worlds," descriptions of massive destruction and chaos as it was occurring in New York City. This, as we now know, was no fabrication. As the day and its devastating events unfolded, I met with my students and found myself asking them what their responses were to the news, what the possible alternatives might be to the "racial prejudice [and] wartime hysteria"[5] that precipitated the internment of Japanese immigrants and their American-born children after the attack on Pearl Harbor and that could be unleashed against other groups as a result of 9/11. As I developed my sabbatical proposal, the parallels and immediate relevance of my research to contemporary events grew suddenly and increasingly evident.

Although the project itself was clearly outlined, the road to Santa Fe, literally and figuratively, was hardly a direct one; it epitomized the roles of disappointment, success, spontaneity, and serendipity in research and the importance of being open to any encounter. In the winter of 2002, I was focusing on learning what I could about Reverend Watanabe's story and traveled to the Island of Hawai'i (also called "the Big Island") to find the Ola'a Japanese Christian Church, where my grandfather had his ministry at the outbreak of the Pacific War. It was from here that he had been seized from his parsonage on December 7, 1941. What remained was an empty lot surrounded by an old moss-covered stone wall. No parsonage. The original building, I learned, had become termite-ridden beyond cost-effective repair, so the church had been rebuilt on another site. Now renamed the Puna United Church of Christ, it is no longer the Japanese Christian church that served primarily *issei* plantation workers, and although Reverend Watanabe's photograph appears on the church's office wall on its roll of ministers, no one could tell me anything about him. The church's seventy-fifth anniversary history did devote five lines to him, some of it erroneous, so I shared with the minister and his secretary what little I knew at that point and later received a ninetieth anniversary bulletin that included a line acknowledging my grandfather's experience during the war. I began to understand on some level the distinction that Pierre Nora makes between history as a "reconstruction . . . a representation of the past" and memory as "always a phenomenon of the present," "in permanent evolution, subject to the dialectic of remembering and forgetting, . . . and capable of lying dormant for long periods only to be suddenly reawakened" (3)—the consequential fragility of that memory. Perhaps my brief visit had inadvertently caused Reverend Watanabe to take on a different presence from the faded photo on the wall or the forgotten lines in the previous church history; perhaps I had caused him to be remembered.

Thanks to friends, I was able to stay at the Kilauea Military Camp, a military recreation area on the Big Island prior to and since World War II and the first facility where, according to my grandfather's notes, he and others from the island were imprisoned. During those clear, sunny days in February 2002, I felt the enormity of the freedom that I assumed I had to come and go as I pleased, in contrast to the men who had been taken there by force over six decades before. Of that time, internee Muin Ozaki wrote:

> As if to relish
> Each step I take
> On this great earth,
> I walk—to the mess hall.
> The only walk allowed.

Leaving the Big Island with little more than a vague sense of the places where my grandfather had been, I was, of course, disappointed but chose perseverance over discouragement. In March 2002, I planned a research trip to Santa Fe devoted to collecting whatever I could on the internment camp and the experience of the Japanese immigrants imprisoned there. Having contacted Joe Ando of the Santa Fe historical marker committee, I received helpful information and encouragement from him and also made plans to meet with him during that time. This fifth trip to Santa Fe became pivotal to my project and launched my study.

Staying with a colleague and friend who supported my research, I worked for days in the New Mexico State Library, getting oriented and searching through vertical files and microfilms, as well as in the New Mexico State Archives next door, which produced various files of correspondence from the governors who had served during the war years. There were many narratives here waiting to be written. I began to imagine some of the possibilities. A tip from Joe Ando also led me to seek out Thomas Chávez, former director of the Museum of New Mexico's Palace of the Governors, whose 1997 newspaper article drew attention to the existence of the camp, and to search the files of the Fray Angélico Chávez Library at the Palace of the Governors. From an address found in a file, I contacted Koichiro Okada, who had written a master's thesis titled "Forced Acculturation" and who kindly gave me a copy of this unpublished work that paid rare attention to the *issei* in the Santa Fe Internment Camp (SFIC) during World War II. Finally, with Joe's directions and the help of strangers, my friend and I were able to find the site of the internment camp, now a thriving housing development.

The cumulative work, especially reading archival documents, book chapters, and journal and newspaper articles, proved invaluable in establishing a foundation on which I could begin to construct scenarios of the Santa Fe internment experience. It also helped me to gain a sense of the past anti-Japanese attitudes in New Mexico, fueled by the large contingent of New Mexicans involved in the Bataan Death March as well as by an evolving sense of Santa Fe's community history. This was a history apparently plagued by divisions and conflicts brought to the fore by the SFIC historical marker project and eventually healed by the courage of a few civic leaders. The only reference to Reverend Watanabe, however, was his name on a roster of SFIC internees that I found on microfilm.

As a result of my commitment to this research and because I was a family member of an internee, Colonel Ando and Dr. Chávez invited me to attend the dedication of the SFIC historical marker just three weeks later. I felt it was a monumental privilege for a researcher in the early stages of a project to be included in an event of such significance. Not only was it to be memorable historically as something long overdue, but I knew it was also of great social and political importance to Santa Feans, having learned of the community strife that had surrounded the establishment of the marker.

And it was indeed a special day. On April 20, 2002, many on a hill in Santa Fe saw the coming together of people of different ethnicities, communities, and generations and their efforts toward a common goal: establishing a stone marker at Frank S. Ortiz Park to recognize the historical fact that during World War II, a U.S. Justice Department internment camp existed on the site of the present Casa Solana neighborhood; to memorialize the experience of thousands of Japanese immigrants and American-born citizens of Japanese ancestry unjustly incarcerated there between 1942 and 1946; and to heal old wounds.

Under an intensely blue and sunny sky, the event was also a baptism of wind and dust for some 250 participants and onlookers—and the marker itself, a large, six-ton granite boulder with a bronze plaque engraved with the following:

> At this site, due east and below the hill, 4555 men of Japanese ancestry were incarcerated in a Department of Justice Internment Camp from March 1942 to April 1946. Most were excluded by law from becoming United States citizens and were removed primarily from the West Coast and Hawaii. During World War II, their loyalty to the United States was questioned. Many of the men held here without due process were long time resident religious leaders, businessmen, teachers, fishermen, farmers, and others. No person of Japanese ancestry in the U.S. was ever charged or convicted of espionage throughout the course of the war. Many of the internees had relatives who served with distinction in the American Armed Forces in Europe and in the Pacific. This marker is placed here as a reminder that history is a valuable teacher only if we do not forget our past.

With loyalty and patriotism being so critically in question sixty years before—and with echoes of those questions so prevalent today in post-9/11 America—the Pledge of Allegiance recited at the ceremony conveyed layers of unspoken meaning. To the crowd of local residents, visitors from places as distant as Alaska, Hawai'i, and Washington, D.C., and honored guests from the state and city, Chávez said, "We are here not to celebrate an event about which none of us is proud; we are here to commemorate an event that happened; it is our history."

The biting wind and dust we felt may not have been so different from the conditions experienced by the men in the SFIC over half a century earlier. Representing the internee families, Joe Ando commented on the self-censorship among these men: "In many Japanese American families across this country, our fathers never spoke to their children about their experiences in the camps. It was a shameful, it was a painful experience." And because of the secrecy surrounding the DOJ facilities, such camps as the SFIC were more misunderstood.

In the late 1990s, due to such historical misunderstandings, some World War II veterans, who confused Japanese immigrants with the Japanese enemy, vehemently protested the proposed marker and caused a significant controversy in the Santa Fe community. In the end, Santa Fe's mayor, Larry Delgado, broke the tie vote of the city council in favor of erecting the marker. A cooperative effort of citizens of different ethnic and racial backgrounds, the establishment of the SFIC marker represented a collective rather than a single ethnic triumph.

I was moved by the attendance of internee families from all over the country and by the social, political, and spiritual gravity of the event. At the luncheon reception following the dedication, Colonel Ando asked me to speak to the crowd, and I surprised myself by overcoming my shyness and addressing the large audience as an intimate one, bound by the common inheritance of internment and, among non–Japanese Americans, the desire not to forget. The attentiveness of this audience brought the gravity of my project home to me. I began to realize my place and the place of my research in relation to the Japanese American community and to the American public at large.

The Road Home: Archival Research, Personal Stories, and Communal Memory

Inspired by the enormity of my charge, I returned to Washington, D.C., where I was serving as a scholar-in-residence at the Smithsonian Institution. With the invaluable mentorship of veteran researchers Aiko Yoshinaga Herzig and the late Jack Herzig, who had assisted the Commission on Wartime Relocation and Internment of Civilians, and of Franklin Odo, director of the Smithsonian Institution's Asian Pacific American Program, months of work at the National Archives—Archives I in Washington, D.C., and Archives II in College Park, Maryland—produced five files on Tamasaku Watanabe: one from the Immigration and Naturalization Service (INS, RG 85), one from the Military Government of the Territory of Hawaii (now RG 494), one from the Department of Justice (including records from the Federal Bureau of Investigation, RG 60), and two from the Office of the Provost Marshal General (RG 389).

Day after day, I dragged my computer bag with laptop and scanner over the rough sidewalks and grassy areas of the National Mall to the historic halls of Archives I or found a desk in the spacious second floor Researcher Room of the contemporary Archives II and pored over hundreds of pages of typed memos and lists, mimeographed forms, and other reports, mostly carbon copies on aging onion skin. Since I did not know my grandfather well, in a sense—very ironically—I began to know him through these files created by his captors. Although many documents overlapped, reflecting the multiple carbon copies produced by the army's bureaucracy, each file came to represent a different view of the man, a somewhat different personality.

The first time I came across his mug shot in the INS file was especially chilling for me as I imagined his humiliation. The degradation of knowing that the authorities would reduce him to two demeaning photographs showed in his hollow stare and grim expression. As I searched through his records and other more general files from the Office of the Provost Marshal General and the State Department, I came across the names of hundreds of others like him—Fujitani, Ikuma, Izutsu, Kato, Kuniyuki, Maehara, Matsumoto, Matsuura, Miho, Ohara, men from Hawai'i, some his friends and acquaintances, many complete strangers, all locked up as he was. All were given the designation "HJ" for Hawai'i Japanese in their civilian internee numbers. Eventually it became clear to me that these men were treated as a discrete group and had a unique experience, being shipped from the Hawaiian Islands over thousands of miles of ocean and land to bone-chilling locations in the northern United States and arid deserts in the Southwest, separated from their families for as many as four years. Rather than studying the broader DOJ incarceration, which by now I saw was massive in scope, I would focus on Reverend Watanabe and the Hawai'i Japanese experience of removal and exile.[6]

In the last months of my stay in Washington, D.C., several incidents occurred that provided another dimension to my text-based project. During a presentation that I gave at the Smithsonian's National Museum of American History, I shared examples of key documents that I had found at the National Archives, among them a petition signed by about two hundred Hawai'i internees. As the documents circulated, there was a small commotion in one corner of the room, and a young woman exclaimed that she had found her great-great-grandfather's signature on the petition. Her father and grandfather would be very interested in speaking with me, she said. This contact eventually led to my first interview a month later in Hawai'i with Edward Ikuma, a veteran of the 100th Battalion, renowned in the European theater during World War II, whose grandfather had been incarcerated with Reverend Watanabe.

Also at the presentation in Washington was Marcia Mau, a grandniece of George Hoshida, who had been taken from the Big Island and who had illustrated people, places, and activities in what seems to be one of the few extant visual records of the DOJ camp experience. She had found a sketch of my grandfather in her copy of her granduncle's memoirs! This was an astounding and precious gift, the first visual image I had seen of him beyond the single photograph of him with his barracks-mates in Santa Fe, found among his records. Knowing that the sketch existed, I could look for the original a year later at the Japanese American National Museum in Los Angeles.

Marcia also told me about Reiko Odate Matsumoto, who lived in the D.C. area and whose father had been taken from the Island of Kaua'i. Meeting Reiko was another gift, for she not only granted me an interview but also shared her father's camp writings with me, the writings of a Buddhist minister who "thought in haiku" and who belonged to the Literary Society of Santa Fe. Reiko in turn told me about Reverend Shingetsu Akahoshi, also a Buddhist minister, who, though not a resident of Hawai'i at the time of his arrest, was a survivor of the internment and was visiting his children in Virginia. She called me one day to ask if I wanted to accompany her to visit him, and although I wasn't at all prepared to conduct an interview in Japanese, I of course said yes. Reverend Akahoshi, a feisty man in his early nineties, was amazingly clear in memory and articulate in speech. He not only remembered my grandfather in Santa Fe but vividly described a brief interaction that he had with him. Another golden moment, more than I could have hoped for. Personal stories were surfacing, the unwritten and spontaneous recollections of internee survivors like Reverend Akahoshi and the memories of the children of internees like Reiko Matsumoto.

Returning to Hawai'i in January 2003, armed with various lists and files from the National Archives, I planned to seek out internees who had made the same journey to the mainland as Tamasaku Watanabe as well as the now-elderly children of internees who may have had recollections and documents from their fathers now gone. One way of learning my grandfather's story was to learn theirs. The question, of course, was how to find them. Again, the theoretical plan would be modified by more productive realities.

Housed in the University of Hawai'i's Center for Biographical Research through the generosity of Craig Howes, its director, and Stanley Shaub, its manager, I called George Akita, professor emeritus of history and a mentor of mine decades before, simply to talk to him about my project and to share the "good stuff" that I'd been collecting. As luck would have it, he was in Honolulu and was duly impressed by my documents and photographs. Things snowballed from there. He introduced me to Tokiko Bazzell, the UH Library's Japan Collection librarian, who coincidentally had begun organizing an exhibit for the sixtieth anniversary of the formation of the 442nd Regimental Combat Team, the Japanese American unit celebrated for its heroism in the European theater.[7] Seeing my artifacts spurred her to invite me to participate in this exhibit, and, having had some museum experience in the past, I agreed to curate Honoring Our Grandfathers: Japanese Immigrants in U.S. Department of Justice Internment Camps, 1941–45. Hours of curatorial work on Reverend Watanabe's papers and artifacts culminated in the following message in April 2003:

> On this auspicious occasion, as we honor the sons of Japanese immigrants who served, fought, and died heroically in the U.S. military during World War II, let us also remember their fathers, grandfathers, and others who were concurrently incarcerated as "alien enemies" in U.S. Department of Justice internment camps. The sense of duty and patriotism exhibited by the sons was often a reflection of the values of their elders.[8]

It was meant as a reminder—to trigger Nora's dormant memory, to create or stimulate a consciousness. Like the memorial in Santa Fe established a year earlier, it was a physical embodiment of cultural memory.

The exhibit led to an invitation to the reception celebrating the opening of the sixtieth anniversary festivities and the several-faceted exhibit, an event that put me in the company of now elderly veterans, some of whose fathers had been interned. Their names were on one of my lists! On this occasion, I met several of them, starting with Reverend Yoshiaki Fujitani, a retired Buddhist bishop, who introduced me to Katsugo Miho, a retired judge, and Akira Otani, a still-active businessman, all of whom agreed to speak with me about their fathers and their visits as young soldiers to their fathers in internment camps like Camp Livingston in Louisiana and SFIC in New Mexico. I was overjoyed at this stroke of luck, especially because I had become fascinated by the social, political, and emotional dimensions of the father-son relationships captured in a government list that I had happened to find. Each interview produced bundles—varying numbers of photos, letters, and other memorabilia in time-weathered envelopes, albums, and cardboard boxes—as did subsequent conversations with other children of internees and surviving elderly internees themselves.

A week later, I gave my first PowerPoint talk at the Center for Biographical Research titled "More Than a Mug Shot: Reconstructing Lives of Japanese Civilian Internees in U.S. Justice Department Concentration Camps." A large crowd squeezed into the center, and I managed to hold the audience's interest with my narrative about Tamasaku Watanabe and the DOJ camp experience. Most notably, Susan Tokairin, a granddaughter of an internee, had seen my library exhibit and came forward with photographs of the Santa Fe camp left by her grandfather. Charlotte Nagoshi, a friend of newfound friends, told me about Kazumi Matsumoto, a one-hundred-year-old internee survivor living in her hometown on the Island of Kaua'i. Although a blurb on my project had appeared in a local community newspaper, yielding two very significant contacts, this word-of-mouth method understandably worked best in the Hawai'i Japanese community; it became a pattern at subsequent events in Honolulu—relatives of internees coming forward or friends telling me about others. Despite my using a formal protocol of questions, the interviews with internees and families of internees often settled into informal and comfortable conversations. I found myself drawn into important relationships and began to feel that more than being a researcher, I was involved in the recovery of my own community's history.

The demonstrated audience interest in my topic led to follow-up events in 2004 and 2005: "Memorials and Memories," a reception and update for the participants in my study and their families, and "Accessing Hawai'i Civilian Internee Files," a workshop for internee families to promote family research on internees, to reciprocate in some way their generosity toward me, and to develop a collective spirit around the project; and two public lectures in Honolulu, including "From Sand Island to Santa Fe," delivered to a standing-room-only crowd held at and co-sponsored by the Japanese Cultural Center of Hawai'i.[9] A dynamic emotional energy seemed to prevail at these events and in the oral history conversations with internees and internee families, with talk serving often to "reawaken" memory. Treasured bundles—photographs, notebooks, letters, journals, plaited bags, paintings, and other forms of material culture—as artifacts not only triggered but also contained that memory, embodied meaning. Some families who had hidden, forgotten, or simply laid aside these stories began to come forward to tell them and, by seeing artifacts valued in exhibits and displays, began to appreciate what they still have. Others I talked with had no writings, no photographs, no records, no memories of any sort until I provided them with copies of documents.

In the process of unbundling and rebundling, what originated as a text-based study of language and literacy has expanded into a multidimensional, multigenerational, multigenre project composed of faces of young men, now old, of fathers, now gone, and of voices speaking through oral histories in the present and material culture of the past. My grandfather's individual life has melded into a community of lives. My personal memory has become communal. And the biography of one man has become a composite of the stories of many of the hundreds of men who, over the course of a sunny morning in December 1941, became "alien enemies" in their country of residence.

Notes

1. United States Immigration and Naturalization Service.
2. On Sunday, December 7, 1941, the Pearl Harbor Naval Base and other military installations on the Island of O'ahu were attacked by planes of the

Imperial Japanese Navy. The United States officially entered World War II on December 8, 1941, by an act of Congress.

3. On August 10, 1936, President Roosevelt wrote a memo to his "Chief of Operations" stating that "every Japanese citizen or non-citizen on the Island of O'ahu who meets these Japanese ships or has any connection with their officers or men should be secretly but definitely identified and his or her name placed on a special list of those who would be the first to be placed in a concentration camp in the event of trouble."

4. A total of 17,477 people were interned by the Department of Justice. The ten more widely known prison camps, such as those at Manzanar and Tule Lake in California, Minidoka in Idaho, and Amache/Granada in Colorado, were established and overseen by the War Relocation Authority as a result of President Roosevelt's Executive Order 9066 issued on February 19, 1942. The WRA and DOJ incarcerations differed in their histories, administrations, prisoners, and treatment of prisoners. See Kashima.

5. The Civil Liberties Act of 1988, signed by President Ronald Reagan forty-three years after the end of the war, offered an apology by the U.S. government on behalf of the nation to surviving American-born Japanese and their immigrant parents who had been incarcerated. The reasons cited were "racial prejudice, wartime hysteria, and a failure of political leadership."

6. "Exile" describes the banishment of Reverend Watanabe and this specific group of seven hundred *issei* from the Hawaiian Islands to the mainland United States. Although the U.S. government erected an internment camp at Honouliuli on O'ahu and several hundred internees of Japanese and, in much smaller numbers, German and Italian heritage were housed there, this group of *issei* was shipped to the mainland in ten boatloads and prohibited from returning to the Islands even after numerous petitions were made to the authorities by individuals and groups and paroles had been granted to some whose sons were serving in the U.S. military. The majority was disallowed from returning until November 1945, three months after the war ended.

7. Although American-born men of Japanese ancestry served in the U.S. armed forces prior to the outbreak of the Pacific War, their status was questioned after Pearl Harbor was attacked, and those who newly volunteered for military service were classified as 4-C—enemy aliens—and prohibited from service. After a "long, arduous, and almost impossible struggle . . . that had to be overcome before the Nisei was restored the right to fight and die for [their] country" (Tsukiyama 15), the government formed the segregated Japanese American 442nd Regimental Combat Team. Together with their predecessors in the 100th or "Purple Heart" Battalion, the first segregated Japanese American unit, the 442nd RCT became the "most decorated mili-

tary unit in American history for its size and length of service" (Crost qtd. in Tsukiyama 19).

8. These are the introductory comments I wrote for a placard posted at the exhibit.

9. I have also presented papers on this topic at several scholarly conferences, nationally and internationally, and have been invited to give presentations to community, university, and public school groups in Honolulu; Albuquerque and Santa Fe; Youngstown, Ohio; and Calgary, Canada, reflecting a widespread interest in the subject.

Works Cited

Clark, Paul F. "Those Other Camps: An Oral History Analysis of Japanese Alien Enemy Internment during World War II." M.A. thesis, California State University, Fullerton, 1980.

Kashima, Tetsuden. *Judgment without Trial: Japanese American Imprisonment during World War II.* Seattle: U of Washington P, 2003.

Nora, Pierre. "General Introduction: Between Memory and History." *Realms of Memory: Rethinking the French Past, Vol. 1.* Ed. Lawrence D. Kritzman. New York: Columbia UP, 1996. 1–20.

Ozaki, Muin. Poem. *Poets behind Barbed Wire.* Ed. and trans. Jiro Nakano and Kay Nakano. Honolulu: Bamboo Ridge, 1983.

Roosevelt, Franklin D. Memo to Chief of (Naval) Operations. Aug. 10, 1936. Box 216, Folder A 8-5, RG 80 (General Records of the Navy Department), National Archives, Washington, D.C.

Tsukiyama, Ted T. *Go for Broke, 1943–1993.* Honolulu: n.p., 1993.

U.S. Government. Civil Liberties Act of 1988. *Civics Online.* 1988. <http://www.civics-online.org/library/formatted/texts/civilact1988.html>.

11

Mississippi on My Mind

W. Ralph Eubanks

"Mississippi Reveals Dark Secrets of a Racist Time," read the headline on the front page of the *New York Times* that March morning. It was 1998, and the files of the once-secret Mississippi State Sovereignty Commission had just been opened. Up until I began to read the *Times* that morning and other newspaper articles throughout the spring of that year, I had never even heard of this thing called the "Sovereignty Commission." Even the name seemed a bit odd, but not out of character with the racially charged history of Mississippi. One thing I did remember was that "sovereignty" was often used as a code word for segregation. It made sense for an organization in Mississippi devoted to maintaining segregation to make use of the coded speech of the era.

When I gazed at that headline, it had been nearly ten years since I had set foot in Mississippi. I was comfortably middle-aged and happy with my life in Washington, D.C., as a southern expatriate. This talk of an organization that spied on its own citizens for the sake of maintaining a segregated society did not engender warm thoughts about the land of my birth, only disdain. Yet the more I read of the Sovereignty Commission, the more intrigued I became with this organization. The numerous news stories I began to devour revealed that the Sovereignty Commission was linked to some of the major crimes of the civil rights era, including the murder of Medgar Evers (it helped with jury tampering in the first trial) and the murder of three civil rights workers in Philadelphia, Mississippi (it held information on those three young men that Neshoba County law enforcement provided to their murderers to track them down). Although unknown to me during my childhood, this thing called the Sovereignty Commission had been authorized to keep integration out of Mississippi at any cost and created a climate of fear and suspicion among blacks and whites.

In the weeks that followed the opening of the Sovereignty Commission files, I noticed a great deal of national coverage about the files in several other major East and West Coast newspapers, in magazines such as *Time, Newsweek,* the *New Yorker,* and the *New Republic,* and across the South. But like many events in American life, once the news cycle surrounding the opening of the secret files was over, the fanfare died down, and awareness of this archive document-ing the culture that created massive resistance to integration in Mississippi fell into the dustbin of cultural amnesia.

Although the Sovereignty Commission was out of the news, I couldn't get it out of my mind. I'd largely separated myself from my home state, but the opening of these secret files that covered most of my life in Mississippi began to draw me back in. I began to read everything I could possibly find on the Sovereignty Commission, amassing a large file of newspaper and magazine articles. And I started to read lots of books about Mississippi: Anne Moody's *Coming of Age in Mississippi*, Willie Morris's *North toward Home*, William Faulkner's *The Sound and the Fury*, the stories of Eudora Welty. As the books began to stack up in my living room, I started talking about Mississippi at the dinner table with my family, trying to engage my children with stories about my home state.

Then, one night at bedtime, my son Patrick asked me, "Daddy, what's Mississippi like?" So I began to tell him about life on my farm, some of my family's lore from those days, but nothing about what Mississippi is really like. Then his brother piped in from the bottom bunk: "Can we go there sometime?" I told them they could but not until they were older. By then, I thought, I would have figured out the answers to my questions about the Sovereignty Commission.

Several months later, I decided to find out if my parents were on the list of 87,000 names I had read about in all those articles on the Sovereignty Commis-sion that dotted my cluttered desktop. At this point, the editor and publisher in me began to ponder a book about the organization, but I was still too afraid to even think about the horrors that might be in the files I had read so much about. It took me until the fall of 1998 to get up the nerve to see if my parents were in the files. When I saw their names on my computer screen, on the Web site of the Mississippi American Civil Liberties Union, I felt like someone had hit me in the stomach, even physically ill. I called my wife, who was traveling at the time, to tell her what I found. She calmed me down and told me to "sit down and write about how you feel right now." And it was really at that moment that my journey began, eventually leading me to return to Mississippi after a ten-year absence with no plans to ever return. It was also at that point that my book began. The first journal entry I made the night after the discovery of my parents' names led me to write the opening line of my book: "The years have a way of providing what seems to be an infinite distance . . ."

Over the next three years, I spent hours pouring over Sovereignty Commis-sion documents in Mississippi's Department of Archives and History as well as exploring related documents in other Mississippi archives. It was through this documentary research that I was able to reconstruct my Mississippi past and reveal a part of it that I never knew existed. In the process of stitching together pieces of my past, the idea for my book moved from the idea of a cultural biography of a segregationist organization into a memoir that wove that cultural biography into its fabric. But getting started on the research for my book, *Ever Is a Long Time*, began in fits and starts and did not go as smoothly as I thought it would.

Months went by after my initial discovery of my parents' names in the Sovereignty Commission files before I could muster up the courage to go and search through those documents. I was truly afraid of what might be lurking in their contents. Because I had not visited Mississippi in ten years or lived there in over twenty, all I had left were cherished recollections of places, people, and childhood that I had reconstructed to comfort me. Would I dare spoil the memories by what I might find in the files? I even asked myself how I could reconcile these two worlds, one I loved and one I looked upon with disgust. I resolved that I wanted to judge what was true about the past. Only then could I bring my two views of Mississippi together.

Before I went to Mississippi, I sent away for the documents that bore my parents' names. The file that arrived in my mailbox a month later seemed relatively innocuous, containing lists of names. However, my parents were not on the same list. Why this happened wasn't clear to me from the material I had received, which left me with the same puzzlement and shock I had felt looking at the ACLU Web site.

Something told me that there was more behind these papers. Exactly how had my parents landed on separate lists? I had to know. After months of restless contemplation, on a fall morning in 1999 I pulled out of my driveway in Washington, D.C., and drove straight to Mississippi to find out why. The next morning, after I walked past the Confederate memorial and up the marble steps into the reading room of the Mississippi Department of Archives and History in Jackson, I spent hours looking at page after page of documents on a computer screen. With blind determination, day after day I searched vigorously to find out why my family was worthy of being watched by the state of Mississippi. This led to a frustrating series of researcher's dead ends and wrong turns. I searched by name, county, town, and even categories such as 'integration agitators." What I discovered during the course of these twists and turns was that parts of the files are closed for reasons of privacy rights. Within the vast files, material exists that I might have found to be personally enlightening, but the main subject of the file has chosen to keep his or her file sealed.

By the end of my first day of research, I was confused, bleary eyed, and frustrated. The random, categorical rather than chronological organization of the Sovereignty Commission files had stretched my researcher's patience. The only thing that I found that really helped me was a manuscript file in a collection on small Mississippi towns marked with the name of my hometown, Mount Olive. In that file was a story about a house that had been "flattened" by a tornado in 1992. I knew this was my old house, because a friend had described its destruction in those very terms. Since my research was going nowhere, I decided to hop in my car, drive to Mount Olive, and take a walk around the old home place to clear my head. Maybe, by going back to where I began, I could start to make some sense out of the barrage of documents that had been staring at me from a computer screen for six hours.

When I arrived on the streets of Mount Olive and began to reacquaint myself with my hometown and its environs, it occurred to me that it was through knowledge of the town that I could begin to make sense of the random snippets of information I found in the files. After I returned to the archives the next day, I did not make much more progress in my research. However, I had come to the realization that I had to combine my sense of place, as well as my connection to the people and places around my hometown, with my research in the archives to make sense of those documents. That realization did not help me on this trip, but it became a guidepost for me on subsequent research trips to Mississippi.

As a small boy, I had traveled every nook and cranny of my hometown and the county with my father, who was then called the "Negro County Agent." After hours of looking up names, dates, and files on a computer screen, they began to come into focus once I started conjuring up the memories of the curious, observant six-year-old boy I had once been. I began to think back to those trips down country roads I had traveled with my father. After pulling up those memories, I remembered names and events I'd forgotten. What had often puzzled me as a child as I wandered through rural Mississippi with a view from the backseat of a 1962 Chevy Bel Air started to make sense, as best as one can make sense of that era in Mississippi's history.

During my research visits, I took more trips down those same country roads. The outings, which brought back even more childhood memories, helped me break through the random nature of the files. But even with this newfound clarity, after a while my research on the computer screens at the Mississippi Department of Archives and History ran into another series of dead ends. I understood the events recounted in the documents and remembered many of the people mentioned in them, yet I had no sense of how the state government may have used the documents. Because the electronic archive of the Sovereignty Commission files was based on a loose series of information categories—for example, names or categories such as integration agitators and freedom schools—a great deal of serendipity governed my research. A conversation with a reporter with extensive knowledge of the files reminded me that although the files had been sealed, their existence became public because random documents turned up in other archives. After this discovery, my search took me to other archives where documents I found, after working through a box of papers in chronological order, helped make sense of what I had found randomly on a computer screen.

At this point in my research, I had filled in details behind my childhood memories from the information on my parents in the files. What I was trying to do now was to find out details from the Sovereignty Commission files about actual historical events of the times and to tie them with the perceptions I had experienced as a child of those same events. Specifically, I was trying to piece together the events of the 1964 Freedom Summer, a summer whose murders, bombings, and burnings had struck fear inside my mind and whose imagery sticks with me to this day. My search took me to the family papers of former Mississippi governor Paul B. Johnson, which contained Sovereignty Commission reports he had received during his term. As I paged through the chronology of Johnson's time as governor from 1964 to 1968, I saw reports from the Sovereignty Commission that had crossed his desk scattered among legislative and political issues, including details of the commission's investigation of the civil rights movement during the summer of 1964. Throughout the summer, there were reports from the commission about the disappearance of the three civil rights workers in Philadelphia, Mississippi: Andrew Goodman, James Cheney, and Michael Schwerner. By the fall, the commission had gone county by county to investigate the aftermath of Freedom Summer, including a visit to the sheriff of Covington County to see if there had been any voter registration schools in the county or any "trouble" from the National Association for the Advancement of Colored People. The document mentioned men who were "working in a quiet way" with the NAACP in and around my hometown. One of those men was my father. For the first time, I realized how the documents I had viewed by subject and place on a computer screen had been actually used by a sitting governor. Now I understood how a personal letter to the governor could launch a Sovereignty Commission investigation of an organization, as I had discovered in the case of my father with the Extension Service, his employer during the period he was placed in the Sovereignty Commission files. I also saw documents I had not seen in the main archives of the Sovereignty Commission in Jackson, a sign that some key pieces of information had probably been destroyed. Much of this missing material included minutes of Sovereignty Commission meetings, which could have provided incriminating information on how the commission discussed the ways it used or could use the information its agents and informants had gathered.

Though there was a flurry of investigations during the summer of 1964 and into the fall, the Sovereignty Commission moved into a period of relative dormancy in its aftermath. The documents I found revealed that Governor Johnson knew that the Sovereignty Commission bore direct responsibility for the Freedom Summer murders. The events of that summer and their tie to Sovereignty Commission investigations even led him by 1965 to proclaim before the U.S. Commission on Civil Rights that Mississippians would accept the Civil Rights Act of 1964 "in a calm, intelligent manner, regardless of personal conviction." From what I could see in his papers, as early as the fall of 1964, Governor Johnson had begun to rethink the role of the Sovereignty Commission. By no means had the murders of Goodman, Cheney, and Schwerner changed the man who "stood tall" against admitting James Meredith to Ole Miss into a racial moderate. But they had forced Johnson to approach his stand on segregation with greater caution.

As I paged through the files that contained material on the aftermath of the murder of the three civil rights workers, another item stood out. It was a one-sentence letter from January 1965, six months after the murders, from a state representative and Sovereignty Commission member that read, "Is Mississippi going to have a Sovereignty Commission?" Governor Johnson replied, "I have felt the need to delay the matter for this period of time." Beginning with a series of recommendations from the director of the Sovereignty Commission, Erle Johnston, I discovered that the governor had been considering whether the commission's investigations were making matters better or worse in Mississippi. The legislator and Sovereignty Commission member who penned this letter was Horace Harned of Starkville, Mississippi, who insisted that Mississippi have a Sovereignty Commission and put forth a resolution demanding the activation of the watchdog group. His spare choice of words to the governor intrigued me. This led me to look into who this Horace Harned was, where he was from, and where he was now. I found out through some digging that he was the last surviving member of the Mississippi State Sovereignty Commission. That meant that I had to talk with him and get his perception of the events of the summer of 1964. After a brief exchange of letters between us, I was soon on my way to Mississippi to meet Harned and get his view of the work of the Sovereignty Commission.

After interviewing Harned, the shape of my book (and my writing) changed. I moved out of working in archives and began interviewing other people. One morning, just two years after my first trip to the archives, I found myself having breakfast with an ex-Klansman, the former superintendent of education in my hometown. His name was Denson Lott, and he was the man who had placed my mother on the list I'd received from the Sovereignty Commission files. In the course of our conversation, Lott revealed to me the identity of the black informants I had read about in the files who had supplied information on civil rights activities to the commission and its representatives. He also displayed a human side that I never expected to find when talking with a former Klansman, who in some ways used our conversation to confess his past sins. He admitted how tangled his life was with Mississippi's racist past, even though that was not the sin he came to me to confess. Again, another piece of the puzzle was put in place, and I decided to weave this story into my narrative.

Next, to understand the politics of the Sovereignty Commission lawsuit and the subsequent turmoil it created in Mississippi's civil rights establishment, I spent hours with Ed King, a former civil rights worker who served as an advocate to keep parts of the files private. Through our conversations, I now understood why I ran into dead ends in the files: if someone wanted his or her file closed, this action closed access to other parts of the files as well. I also learned firsthand how access to these once-secret files had both opened Mississippi's closed society and sown seeds of division among the very people who had been spied on by the state of Mississippi. Once again, this connection with a person, combined with additional research, reshaped yet another piece of my narrative. Each of these people provided a link to a past that I remembered fleetingly as a child, had become exposed to as an adult through the Sovereignty Commission files, and was now trying to make relevant to the present.

In the course of three years, the archives served as only one component of my journey to find out how my parents ended up in the Sovereignty Commission files. But had it not been for the archives, I would not have been drawn back into the very soul of Mississippi: its people and places. It was through rediscovering the people and places I knew and loved as a boy that my research and writing began to come together. It has also now led me to dig deeper into my family's past, particularly the life of my grandparents, who were an interracial couple in southern Alabama in the 1920s and 1930s. I have few written records to draw on to reconstruct the life of my grandparents but have developed skills at gathering oral history through some of my work on my first book as well as through my involvement in a community "write-a-story" day encouraging ordinary citizens of Washington, D.C., to write down their stories and memories.

In the end, this search sharpened my skills as a researcher and led me to understand that the best stories are often hidden in the places where you least expect to find them. It also rekindled a love of my home state that had been dormant for twenty years. That love began more than forty years ago as I glanced at the scenery from the backseat as I rambled through dusty country roads with my father. Fortunately, much of the scenery looks the same on those country roads as it did when I was a boy. I'm sure that helped my memories come back stronger. What also helped was suppressing that childhood yearning to be in the front seat rather than in the back. Once I started to reconnect with that childhood view from the backseat, my archival research began to make sense. Sometimes a backseat view can provide a window to the world.

Works Cited

Harned, Horace H., Jr. Letter to Paul B. Johnson Jr. January 25, 1965. Paul B. Johnson Papers, folder 2, box 137. Archives and Manuscript Department, William D. McCain Library and Archives, University of Southern Mississippi, Hattiesburg.

Johnson, Paul B., Jr. Letter to Horace H. Harned Jr. February 1, 1965. Paul B. Johnson Papers, folder 2, box 137. Archives and Manuscript Department, William D. McCain Library and Archives, University of Southern Mississippi, Hattiesburg.

12

Dreaming Charles Eastman
Cultural Memory, Autobiography,
and Geography in Indigenous
Rhetorical Histories

Malea Powell

This is a story.[1]

The version of the story you're reading began as a ghost story told out loud around kitchen tables, on porches, at powwows, in archives. It's important to begin with this bit of knowledge, I think, because when talk turns into text, something happens to it—something else arises as the words get inscribed, revised, polished, distressed, and re-presented. Some meanings open and flower; other meanings die the quiet death of alphabet, of print. So in retelling this story this way, I will struggle with the meaning of things, with what we would call in our scholarly way the epistemology of the letter, literally, of the alphabet of the language in which I write, or with what we could also call the thingness of meaning—the effects of the marks (on computer now but eventually on paper) made, and their making, on meaning. All of which is, at best, an odd way to say that this is a text best read out loud.

This story comes, as all stories do, from a much larger, more complicated accumulation of stories. While some of you, dear readers, may be familiar with my persistent scholarly desires to listen to late-nineteenth-century American Indian intellectuals like Sarah Winnemucca Hopkins (Northern Paiute), Charles Alexander Eastman (Santee Dakota), Susan LaFlesche Picotte (Omaha), and Andrew Blackbird (Harbor Springs Ojibwe/Odawa), what I have been charged to do here is to look critically at my experiences as archivist and composer of these rhetorical histories. When I accepted that charge, I promised that I'd do so by looking through the constellated lenses of cultural memory, autobiography, and geography and that I would work through this aporia in the imagined presence of my own esteemed teachers, mentors, colleagues, and students. I am going to try to fulfill those promises, then, through a series of scenes. Each scene arises from the physical space of an archive, a location of deliberate institutional cataloging of memory. Each scene is a story, a narrative strand in the braid of "how to do" indigenous rhetorical history, how to live with the ghosts of that doing. Each scene is both the beginning and the end of a methodology, a remembered fragment of a battle in what Gerald Vizenor has called "the Word Wars."[2]

While many scholars in Native studies take for granted the meaning of that phrase "the Word Wars," others may have less access to the complexities of meaning caught in its figurative jaws. What we are talking about is a collusion of events during colonization—the documents and histories written *about* Native peoples by folks who had something to lose if Indians were seen as fully human, the laws and treaties that authorized brutality and genocide in all of the Americas, the forced learning of English at the hands of missionaries and in boarding schools, the continuing devaluement of the oral for the written (or the virtual), and the continuing ignorance of most U.S. citizens about the story of colonization and of imperialism and its continuing consequences. We are still in the midst of this war, still living through a paracolonial occupation, and the damage done by documents, by words, has been at least as great as that done by weapons. This is why I have spent many years collecting documents by, about, for, and from American Indians. My own particular obsession (my, er, scholarly focus) is with documents from a time period that would convention-ally be described as beginning with the Civil War until the New Deal (about 1861 until about 1934). For Native peoples, and certainly for Native scholars, this same time period can be thought of as beginning shortly after Removal, encompassing much of the spectacular brutality of the nineteenth-century Indian Wars and the Allotment Era, including the Boarding School Era, and ending with the Indian Reorganization Act (the Indian New Deal).

But ways of naming/marking "history" aren't what I want to talk about here in this story about being an archivist and composer of indigenous rhetorical histories.[3] What it all comes down to is that like many students of history, I've spent time in a lot of libraries, a lot of archives. Besides their participation in the larger imperial project of "collecting knowledge," many of these spaces had some mundane things in common—the way they smelled, the hard wooden chairs, my own weird disorientation after spending hours at their microfilm machines, and the general set of writing rituals that scholars were expected to perform if they wanted access to materials. Access required knowledge of a very specialized type: how to find and identify the documents within catalogs and holdings lists and finding guides, and to do so in such a way that your simple request would pass unimpeded through the system's many gatekeepers; how to fill out forms, pay for things, use the physical space of the archive—all of these an elaborate maze each time I visited someplace new, all designed to keep the knowledge safe, protected, away from the prying eyes of the uninitiated and the uninformed.

But access isn't what I want to talk about here either—though I will want to do so someday—and the project of the imperial archive in the Americas is also something that is simply beyond the scope of my work here in *this* document (though, again, in the discipline of rhetoric and composition, there will be a time when we will need to talk about that as well). My point here is what it feels like to be in an archive, not because I think you care how *I* feel but to illustrate the ways in which meaning is sometimes held captive by the body and how we have to then walk through story to make sense of our experiences as writers, as scholars, and as humans. Some events have to be walked and talked aloud, moved through, *told*. As Cherokee scholar and poet Qwo-Li Driskill has recently pointed out, "The archival project was not created *for* Indians. It was created to consolidate knowledge *about* Indians. And yet, here I am, an Indian in the archive" (1). And here *I* am, an Indian talking about what it means to be an Indian in the archive, what it means to be the object looking back, the objectified engaged in the process of making knowledge about the processes that led to my objectification. And, more truthfully, I'm not sure I can tell you what it means—what I hope these scenes tell you is how it feels, and how out of that feeling comes both methodology and story.

Scene One

I'm at the Saint Louis University Law Library. It's summer in St. Louis—July—damp and hot, deeply uncomfortable to be outside. The library's cool interior seems to offer a respite from that discomfort, and I am grateful that my plans for the day are to spend at least ten hours working with the library's Native American Reference Collection. The collection comprises seventy-six microfilm reels that include approximately 5,500 congressional documents, reports, and committee hearings supplemented by some 2,500 pamphlets, annual reports, and other materials published by private and non-congressional government sources from 1840 to 1948; these documents, collected by agents of the Bureau of Indian Affairs starting in 1870, were used for the BIA's in-house research and cover nearly every aspect of the agents' surveillance and documentation of American Indian life as they saw it. I spent four days working my way through the collection.

On the fourth day, I stood on the steps of the library in dread. My joints ached with the osteoarthritis-mimicking symptoms of stress; my knees creaked up the stairs; my shoulders already slumped at the prospect of entering what now seemed an icy cell in which I was to be tormented by the words on the microfilm reader's screen, by the material force that those words recollected, represented, produced, and replicated on the bodies of Native peoples—mine included. Don't get me wrong—the people I met at the library were exceedingly pleasant and helpful. The librarians were friendly and supportive of my work; they "held" the best microfilm reader/printer for me every day; they let me make thousands of pages of microfilm copies for free; they pointed out good places to eat and have coffee; they prompted me to take a break periodically. It wasn't the people in that place that tore at me and filled the articulated bones in my body with inflammation; it was the words, the writing, the documents, and their presence in that place that ate at me, pounded inside my head, and roared through my body like a freight train. I went back to my hotel room each night, my stomach clenched against the sharp space that had been carved out of me. I filled that space with other sounds—the voice of Daryl Baldwin Jr. on a Miami language tape I'd brought with me, the Twigh Twee Singers singing "Siipioncii," from the river, the place of life, and my daughter on the phone wondering when I'd be coming home. I returned to the library each day to be excavated by the words of people who believed that me, and mine, were worthless . . . savages . . . lazy . . . violent . . . and, quite simply, *in the way*—I returned because I was learning how much those words mattered, still matter.

Finally, at the end of all of that, I went to stay with my friend Drucilla Wall, a mixed-blood Muscogee poet and scholar. Lounging lazily on her sunlight-filled front porch, I listen to Dru's words; she reminds me of what I knew-but-had-forgotten in that archive—if you feel written on, write back. So, this is my first attempt at writing back to that archive. This is a poem, a bridge, cross it out loud.[4]

LISTING

Part One—how they did it

"A Message from the President of the United States
concerning . . .
                Citizenship in the Indian Nations
                Free Homesteads on Public Lands
                Indians Who Served in the Army of the United States
                What the Government and the Churches are doing for
                the Indian"

"A Letter from the Secretary of the Interior
concerning . . .
                the Rules for Governing the Court of Indian Offenses
                the Organization of the Territory of Oklahoma

Blankets for the Indian Service
Indian Depredation Claims"

"In the Senate of the United States: a report
concerning . . .
          the Sale of Intoxicants to Indians
          the Sale of the Sac & Fox Reservation
          the Utah and Northern Railway Company
          Correspondence on the Subject of Teaching the Vernacular
          in Indian Schools"

This is how they did it.
This is how they   filed   us   down
          to words
          printed on papers
          stamped and signed and kept in steel boxes.

25 reels of microfilm per collection,
          hundreds of documents per reel
                              not just   blankets and guns,
                                        disease and lies,
but   pages and
                    pages and
                         pages.

Part Two—how we undo it

The Physical and Spiritual Realm   *how the world holds together*
     kookáni, spoon (physical)   *maálhsi*, knife (physical)
          alénia, man (spiritual)   *mitémhsa,* woman (spiritual)
               ahpwaakáni, ordinary pipe (physical)
                         ahpwaakána, ceremonial pipe (spiritual)

Verbs   *the center of the People*
     pyaayaáni, I come
     pyaayáni, you come
          iiyaayaáni, I go
          iiyaayáni, you go
                    pyaayani-nko, are you coming?
                    ayaayani-nko, are you going?

All Our Relations
     nimehshoóma, my grandfather   *noohkóma*, my grandmother

noóhsa, my father   *nínkya*, my mother
nihseénsa, my brother   *nimíhsa*, my sister

niihkaána, my friend

paahkinantó ahkwaanteémi, open the door
teépahki neeyólaani, it is good to see you

ceeki neehahki eeweemakiki, all my family is well

iilaataweeyankwi, we speak such a language
weamyaamiki, we miami people

*iilaataweeyankwi, iilaataweeyankwi, iilaataweeyankwi, iilaataweeyankwi
weamyaamiki*

Scene Two

It is several years later. It is summer in Chicago, and I am at the Newberry Library. The Newberry is a magnificent Gilded Age romanesque-revival edifice built nearly on the shores of Lake Michigan on the land that Miamis once called *checagou*, the place of wild garlic.[5] I am sitting at one of the long, cool tables in the reserved reading room, feeling letters written by Charles Eastman from Matotee Lodge, Ontario, in September 1930. No, I didn't make a mistake with the verb in that last sentence. I'm not reading or looking at these letters in the traditional sense—I've already made my request for copies, so I take my task as one in which I simply sit and think and feel in relation to the materials at hand. I admitted to myself a long time ago that part of learning to listen to scholarly elders like Eastman was also learning to listen to myself, to my relatives, to the land, and to the marks written on the land. I sat with those letters for a long time, watching handwriting emerge from the page, thinking about the Newberry's hold on these materials, on the way that I'd been trained to think about archives and the objects they contained, spent a good deal of time thinking through my ethical relationship to *this* archive, to the project of imperial archives, to all the objects stored in all the archives all over the world. As I sat there and thought about empire, I started to get very cold—felt myself grow puny and insignificant in the face of imperialism and shivered at the impossibility of it all—me, an Indian, a mixed-blood, here in this odd colonial space.

It was the appearance of Eastman himself, stepping from a photograph on the table beside me, that broke my intellectual chill.[6] He simply appeared, unfolding from the flat plane of that photograph as I felt myself unfold and emerge from the singularity of that imperial narrative, the one that is so distracting, so seductive that it had me momentarily convinced of its power and speculating on the necessity of abandoning my responsibilities as a human in this world. Eastman's appearance convinced me to run, so I packed up my things and left the building. As I rushed up Clark Street in the bright summer sun, I kept thinking—*What am I supposed to learn from this?* Here's a piece of what I came up with:

Though the Newberry and other buildings like it are textual spaces designed to intimidate, I believe they do so as a way to negate their own temporality and impermanence, and they accomplish that negation through *the practice of history*. Michel deCerteau claims that the practice of history is a symbol of a society capable of managing the space it provides for itself; the power of that society to manipulate space allows it to appear to manage time by changing the practices of the past into a blank page on which the textual product of "the present" can be written. In this same way, these large Gilded Age buildings like the Newberry manage the physical place upon which the imperial society they represent has engaged in empire into a space of argument for the value of Western culture. The land on which the Newberry Library is built is land where Miamis hunted, gathered, and celebrated long before any city was built there, so a reciprocity of relations has long existed between that land and my ancestors. What this means is that the significance of my experiences there *do not* begin in colonization; instead, my ancestral obligation to and alliance with the land are the central practices through which my presence there is negotiated. So, whether harvesting wild garlic or Eastman's writings, in that geographical space, I am engaging in an already established alliance with the physical and emotional needs of the land, an alliance that requires care, respect, and gift-giving for the things that I take away. And because the land, at least, remembers its obligations, I needed to remember, and honor, mine. One of the things that Eastman's impossible reappearance made clear is that neither his letters nor the garlic gathered by my ancestors are simply available objects; no, they are alive, and their harvest requires the appropriate gestures of respect, friendship, honor, and goodwill. Just because Eastman's writings have been made into objects by a story told about them in imperial discourse doesn't mean that we can't, that I can't, tell different stories about them, with them, through them—and the fact of empire doesn't relieve me of my human obligation to their continued existence. History isn't a dead and remembered object; it is alive and it speaks to us. We are obligated not just to our ancestors out of whose lives we "make" that history but also to the places and spaces, and the living things therein, who remember them and—through them—remember us. My obligation to the land, my obligation to Eastman, they are both a part of the same tradition that requests only that I carry the past into the lived present in a respectful and honorable way. As Driskill puts it:

> Cherokees had our own [version of the] Ghost Dance. Like Wovoka's Ghost Dance, it had as its vision the hope for protection from European invasion, the coalitioning of Native nations, and the preservation and continuance of Indigenous lifeways and traditions. Sitting in the archive, touching books my ancestors may have touched, feels like a Ghost Dance. The library throngs with (g)hosts. (1)

But what does that mean for those of us here in this text today?

Scene Three

It is just a few years later. I am in a classroom in a building on the campus of Michigan State University, founded in 1855 as the prototype for the sixty-nine subsequent land-grant institutions that would be established through the Morrill Act of 1862.[7] I am teaching a graduate-level seminar in the theory and methodology of American cultural rhetorics. One of the tasks I'd put forward for this seminar was to, in fact, define what we might mean when we say "American cultural rhetorics." While I won't spread out the breadth of that definition here, I will say that questions of "story" and "history" were central to our meaning-making. And I'll tell this final story about how we began to articulate the connections between story-telling and history-telling, a practice that took recognizable form as we taught each other how to make theory from LeAnne Howe's essay "The Story of America: A Tribalography" alongside Michel deCerteau's book *The Writing of History*. In this seminar, each participant wrote a response to each week's readings. Chad O'Neill, a Mexican American student and multimedia designer, opened his response by commenting on the "differing *storied* openings of the two readings" (1). He then went on to situate these stories alongside one another, first with a quote from Howe:

> When the foreigners arrived and attempted to settle in the upper Northeast, they had nothing to eat, nothing to sustain them but their faith in biblical stories. Indigenous people told them new stories of how to live in our world. (29)

He follows with a quote from deCerteau that recollects a seventeenth-century Dutch etching in which Amerigo Vespucci "discovers" the nude Indian body of "America":

But what was really initiated here is a colonization of the body by the discourse of power. This is *writing that conquers*. It will use the New World as if it were a blank "savage" page on which Western desire will be written. (xxv)

O'Neill then writes: "The conflict implied between these two *encounters* I take not only as interesting, but also as important to the articulation of possibilities. . . . What is between these two stories? What will, in fact, make these possibilities 'thinkable'?" (1–2).

O'Neill shifts the question from "story versus history" to the story *in* history, to the articulated nature of imperial and indigenous discourses, from the impossibility of sustaining "our story" *in the face of* "their story" to the possibility of a shared understanding of story that erupts in various histories. In doing so, he points to space in which the relationships and encounters that I have been trying to tell here take place—the space "between" those articulations, the interstices of emotion, the feeling of what happened. It's not that O'Neill's words tell us something we didn't know; in fact, it's precisely the opposite. His story speaks what we feel, shapes it into a critical question that we could use to bring those feelings to bear in a way that might "make theory."

And here I am now, finishing my story with his story in order to respectfully mark the possibilities that we all can bring to light for one another through story, to raise the questions that came out of that encounter, which I hope I've begun to answer in these pages: What is thinkable for all of us who "do" indigenous rhetorical history? How is that different for Native scholars? For non-Native scholars? What lies between those two spaces of making? What is possible for scholars of color who engage in the process of decolonization by immersing ourselves in the ugly trenches dug by the material and textual shovels of the colonial project? What stories stand between thinkable and possible? How can we learn to tell them? What academic stories have each of us learned to let stand between us as borders, as canyons, as bridges, as homes? How can we learn to tell through them? What are the consequences of "writing back," of thinking back, of taking back in all of this telling? And, for me, how to end *this* story? I'm clearly not nearly "done" with the scholarly issues here, haven't even really begun clearly articulating a methodology. But I am at the end of this story, a narrative that recounts—that tells—in an effort to *mean* affectively. So, I'll leave with another poem. Another bridge. Cross it, again, out loud. Let me know what happens when you get to the other side.

REAL INDIANS
the real indian leans against
the counter at the white castle just off I-65 two miles south of the pow-

wow grounds alongside wapaashiiki, the wabash river whose sycamored
banks and water pitted caves whisper the voices of my elders
but we are here now, not there,
and here is next in line staring out at the parking lot piece-quilted with
trucks and cars and campers, the last space surprised by that listing
Winnebago, y'know, that Ho-Chunk guy who still smells like the last
lonely piece of frybread those Santa Clara guys finally got rid of halfway
through the last giveaway
or maybe
here isn't here at all, but there, at the drive-thru ordering a PakASak of
30 with cheese plus some chicken rings and onion petals to go, to keep us
company on that long drive across I-80—Lake Michigan, the Illinois, the
Mississippi, the Iowa, the Missouri, the Platte
all those rivers, all those miles of hiway on fire, the land twisted black
like winter wind, the sky a smear of pink cotton candy stuffed into the
greedy mouth of a white man whose teeth grind us into the plains
or maybe
what I hear is a mourning song, one that sounds exactly like an orange
tiger cat crying, trying to claw her way out of her lavender-plastic, seat-
belted cage, you know, that song I sing every time we get too far away
from Miami land and Meier stores and French & Indian war monuments
and A & W rootbeer stands open only in the summer and the sound of
the Twigh Twee singers as they warm up before first grand entry and the
way that white castles
never
taste
when you buy them frozen, no peeling away the warm gooey bun from
the steamed meat center to add hot mustard and pickles before you eat
them in three bites and twelve bites later are too drunk with grease to eat
anymore
or maybe
what I hear when i'm here is the sound of us not dying or disappearing,
just eating and talking and laughing and driving,
remembering who we are

Notes

1. I offer my thanks: (*1*) to Victor Villanueva and Gail Okawa, whose generous mentorship and intellectual interests prompted the first oral version of this
story at the 2005 Conference on College Composition and Communication
in San Francisco; (*2*) to the indigenous peoples of central California—the

numerous tribal nations upon whose lands the cities in that area have been built—for allowing this story to be told respectfully on their lands; (*3*) to Gesa Kirsch and Liz Rohan for their patience and persistence; (*4*) to Leonora Smith, Laura Julier, and Julie Lindquist for their careful reading and vital friendship; and (*5*) to my elders for their teachings and their encouragement. What I do well is to their credit; what I do badly belongs only to me.

2. See Vizenor's *Wordarrows: Indians and Whites in the New Fur Trade* for a further articulation of this term and the theoretical matrix in which it was originally used.

3. The ways in which historical narratives are characterized by named events is, of course, one of the results of particular traditions of making history, of making scholarship. While Native studies scholars participate in those ways of making, we do so through different named events. These "namings," of course, also signify what the history-maker deems to be significant and important for the narrative. So, while narratives of "American" history often erase Native peoples (and much of the history of Indian-white relations), the narratives of "Native" history almost always focus on the intercultural relationships that, in fact, created the United States as a physically/landed entity and as a mythology. While this is in itself a fascinating story, it is beyond the scope of this essay.

4. This is a found poem—a rearrangement and reframing of words and phrases taken from archival sources and from Baldwin's Miami language workbook.

5. Before the French arrived in Green Bay in 1634, Native people had lived in the Chicago area for over ten thousand years. Before that, twenty thousand years ago, the Chicago area was covered by a continental glacier—nothing is known about the humans who may have occupied this area before the glacier. The first artifacts of human occupation from this area after glaciation are worked pieces of elk antler dating to about 12,000 B.C., which would indicate that humans were in the area shortly after the glacier began its retreat. The meltwater of its recession would become Lake Michigan. Archaeologists would tell a story about Paleo-Indians, Early Woodland, Middle Woodland, and Late Woodland peoples followed by Mississippians (black-grit potters and tempered shell potters) and then the beginning of the "historical" period—i.e., the coming of the French to Green Bay in 1634. They would also say that they can document, through Marquette and Jolliet's 1673 explorations, that the Miamis were in the Chicago area and that they were later joined by Potowatomis, then displaced by Anishinaabes and Odawas, all of whom ended up in Michigan and became known as the People of the Three Fires. Miamis, of course, were spread to the south and east, all the way to southeastern Ohio. (See Lace.) What Native people will tell you is that the Chicago area was a popular summer residence, especially for

Miami and Illinois tribal groups. We planted there (corn, beans, and squash), gathered there (wild garlic and other herbs and roots), and hunted there (buffalo especially, who ran the Illinois plains in the summer months). (See also Peterson; and Straus, "Found Mothers.") For more information about precontact indigenous cultures and geographies in North America, see Kehoe's *America before the European Invasions.* For more information regarding the etymology of "Chicago," see Vogel's *Indian Place Names in Illinois* and Swenson's "Chicagoua/Chicago: The Origin, Meaning and Etymology of a Place Name."

6. Charles Alexander Eastman was born as Ohiyesa in 1858 on the Santee Sioux (Dakota) reservation in Minnesota. He fled with some relatives to Canada after the Great Sioux Uprising of 1862—his father was one of the Dakotas who fought in that war and was one of 265 Santees when they converted to Christianity (38 who refused to convert were hanged for their participation in the uprising—the largest public hanging in U.S. history). It was as a result of that experience that Eastman was sent to attend Euro-American schools. In November 1890, at the age of thirty-two, he was appointed physician at the Pine Ridge Agency, South Dakota, and by January 1891 was caring for those who had survived the massacre at Wounded Knee. By 1893, Eastman was publishing essays in magazines like *Nicholas* and *Harpers*, and by the time of his death from a heart attack in 1939, he had published dozens of essays and eleven books. His accomplishments are impressive and well beyond the scope of this essay. For more information about Eastman's life and writings, see his own works and Wilson's *Ohiyesa, Charles Eastman, Santee Sioux.*

7. Signed by Abraham Lincoln on July 2, 1862, the Morrill Act granted thirty thousand acres of land for each member of Congress assigned to the state as of the 1860 census. The land, or proceeds from its sale, was to be used to establish and fund educational institutions that would teach military tactics, engineering, and agriculture.

Works Cited

Baldwin, Daryl, Jr. *Iilaataweeyankwi, Lesson One.* Self-published, 1995.

deCerteau, Michel. *The Writing of History.* Trans. Tom Conley. New York: Columbia UP, 1988.

Driskill, Qwo-Li ."Indian in the Archive." Unpublished paper. Feb. 21, 2005. Used with permission.

Howe, LeAnne. "The Story of American: A Tribalography." *Clearing a Path: Theorizing the Past in Native American Studies.* Ed. Nancy Shoemaker. New York: Routledge, 2002. 29–50.

Kehoe, Alice Beck. *America before the European Invasions.* New York: Longman, Pearson Education, 2002.

Lace, Ed. "Native Americans in the Chicago Area." Strauss 23–27.

O'Neill, Chad. Untitled. Unpublished paper. Feb. 21, 2005. Used with permission.

Peterson, Jacqueline. "The Founding Fathers: The Absorption of French-Indian Chicago, 1816–1837." Strauss 31–66.

Strauss, Terry. "Found Mothers: Indian Women in Early Chicago." Strauss 67–81.

———, ed. *Native Chicago*. Chicago: McNaughton and Gunn, 1998.

Swenson, John. "Chicagoua/Chicago: The Origin, Meaning and Etymology of a Place Name." *Illinois Historic Journal* 84 (Winter 1991): 235–48.

Vizenor, Gerald. *Wordarrows: Indians and Whites in the New Fur Trade*. Minneapolis: U of Minnesota P, 1987.

Vogel, Virgil. *Indian Place Names in Illinois*. Pamphlet series 4. Springfield: Illinois State Historical Society, 1963.

Wilson, Raymond. *Ohiyesa, Charles Eastman, Santee Sioux*. Urbana: U of Illinois P, 1983.

13

Cultural Memory and the Lesbian Archive
Kate Davy

> When confronted with the big questions and surprising obstacles of what
> it means to be women in the theater, we did what we had to do. We took
> off our hats and danced.
>
> —Lois Weaver, "Afterword," in
> *The Routledge Reader in Gender and Performance*

On a winter night in 1984, I encountered the WOW Café Theatre for the first
time in its storefront home on East 11th Street in Manhattan's East Village.
The show was Alice Forrester's *Heart of the Scorpion*, billed as a "romance for
the girls." On the same evening, I walked a few blocks farther east to catch
the late show at Club Chandalier, a venue that—like WOW (Women's One
World)—was part of an exciting if short-lived phenomenon known as the East
Village club scene. There, another WOW artist, Alina Troyano, was performing her ersatz lesbian television talk show billed as *Carmelita Tropicana Chats*
and featuring yet other WOW performers as guests. What I discovered that
evening was a different kind of "women's theater," a theater that had managed to carve out a discursive space in representation for women *as subjects* in
productions so alternative to mainstream theater that they staged no less than
the (as yet) unimaginable. I had been a student and scholar of avant-garde
performance for many years, awaiting the consciousness-altering experience it
promised. For me, this little women's theater had blown the lid off this agenda,
productively altering ingrained patterns of thought and emotion without
sacrificing women as autonomous subjects to an avant-garde representational
economy that unconsciously and repeatedly objectified them. At WOW, cut-
ting-edge feminist theory was made flesh. And it was thrilling.

Since then, much has been written by scholars and critics about the work
of WOW artists, and five collections of WOW work have been published
(Hughes; Five Lesbian Brothers; Hart; Troyano; Case). In recent years, I
undertook the project of writing a book about the theater itself on the premise
that its material conditions and ideological context shaped the unique aesthetic
emerging from it. WOW is both a place and a player in the extraordinary

work made possible by its existence. Because a better understanding of any enterprise can be gleaned from its origins and early history, I began by returning to WOW's founding moment—two exceptionally ambitious international women's theater festivals.

Shortly after attending WOW's twentieth anniversary celebration in December 2000, I set out to learn about events I had not attended—WOW's inaugural Women's One World international festivals presented in the fall of 1980 and 1981. The idea was to explore the ways in which these events mirrored the period's feminist theories and aesthetics. I presumed the five hours of short pieces that made up the anniversary celebration would demonstrate, by comparison, how far feminist performance had progressed over the years. Instead, what I learned about WOW's origins did not fit a narrative of progress neatly culminating twenty years later in smarter, more evolved performances. On the contrary, the cultural memory I sought was archived in the performances and spirit of that anniversary night, but I had not recognized it. In her review of the event for the *Village Voice*, Alisa Solomon describes WOW historically as a place where "now well-known artists honed their craft, giving birth to a feminist-and-tinsel-tinged queer aesthetic." A contemporary example of this queer aesthetic would be the drag king act performed that evening by an as-yet-unknown black artist named Dred. It was inconceivable to me then that any precedent for Dred's sexy, crossed-dressed striptease could be found two decades earlier in the context of feminist performance.

While accounts of the festivals vary predictably among the many women who shared their recollections with me, I was struck by a recurring sentiment. To a person, those who attended the festivals described them as having exceeded by far anything they had previously experienced. "I'd never seen anything like it before; there had never *been* anything like it before," was a typical remark. Yet, nearly everyone was frustrated in her attempt to support claims of unparalleled status for WOW's festivals. Most felt the reasons they gave—even as they were giving them—did not capture what was so astonishing about the experience. Among the most common reasons were the festivals' international dimension, the opportunity to see women's theater, and the visibility of some identifiably lesbian work. On the face of it, then, WOW's festivals were not particularly unique. Yet women with disparate backgrounds and experiences concur that there was a felt *something* that made WOW's festivals terribly special, something that cannot be accounted for entirely by the fact of an international women's theater festival on an American shore, or even by the presence of some work with recognizably lesbian content.

C. Carr provides a case in point. If anyone was positioned to consider WOW's festivals as part and parcel of the larger sociopolitical and aesthetic landscape, it is Carr. She was an active participant in the East Village art, performance, and punk rock scenes at the end of the 1970s and would go on to become one of the most well known and respected writers to chronicle East Village performance. Carr, too, recalls that something about WOW's festivals felt extraordinary at the time; and like many others, she has difficulty putting her finger on precisely why this was so. "It seemed so fresh," she recalls, "so different, so exciting. There was a sense of energy to it that most feminist events just didn't have." In the absence of specifics, the *feeling* that produced this deeply held conviction clearly persists in collective memory.

I turned to the Lesbian Herstory Archives in hopes of finding something written about the festivals. This effort required traveling to Brooklyn where the archives fill a brownstone building sandwiched between other brownstones on a typical neighborhood block. Lacking the resources to properly catalogue its holdings, the staff could do little but point me in the direction of a few boxes marked "WOW" or "women's theater." Into these boxes had been tossed, in no particular order, press releases, programs, scripts, copies of opening night reviews, videotapes of some productions, and a smattering of photographs. Archival work in my case resembled more of an archaeological dig—mining memories and boxes of stuff, carefully examining disparate bits and pieces of a whole, widely scattered and deeply buried. Ironically, the events I was trying to reconstruct and understand had taken place only twenty years earlier and the key participants were more than willing to share with me their memories of events and interpretations of what happened. Ultimately, I found more than I was looking for—the dynamics of archival work threw into relief the very nature of cultural memory, revealing painful erasures that ensue from an inevitable, ongoing process of forgetting.

Rifling through the material was simultaneously pleasurable and disheartening. Because WOW is essentially "community theater," that is, nonprofessional theater, few productions were reviewed by critics over the years. What remains of them exists in these boxes, in the personal files of their creators, and in the memories of those who attended. Given the dearth of press coverage, then, I was amazed to find that a number of local publications covered the festivals, some extensively. Someone (or a few someones) had the foresight to clip these articles at the time and subsequently deposit them in the archive. With the exception of the *Village Voice* and the *Advocate*, most of the publications where these pieces appeared are now defunct, and each exists on a continuum of relative obscurity—with the *Soho Weekly News* on one end, *Big Apple Dyke News* (B.A.D. News) on the other, and *Womanews* somewhere in between. Like lived memory, every source of information was incomplete; taken together, however, a whole began to take shape.

Reading descriptions of festival performances written at the time they were presented was compelling and made clear two things in particular: 1) an intense, raw enthusiasm for what each reviewer experienced, and 2) a few performances utterly incongruous with current notions of what constituted feminist cultural production in the 1970s and 1980s. As I read through pieces devoted to the festivals, a kind of tape loop began running through my head—I kept thinking, "This is extraordinary. How could anyone actually *there* then forget *this?*" Those who attended the festivals remember them as astonishing because they were. Deb Margolin, who at the time of the second festival in 1981 was new to both theater and feminism, described her experience in a 2001 interview with me. She recalled, "It was exhilarating. I'd never been so alive and in a cultural community where the criterion for great theater was the passionate desire to speak. And here it was. I watched it roll in like the storm from the water. It was fantastic." This sense of a storm rolling in over the water captures the feeling I had sitting in the archive, up to my elbows in stuff, as I began to make meaning out of that which eluded me. I sensed something important but amorphous coming into focus; it was visceral. Like an archaeologist, I was beginning to unearth pieces of what was so deeply buried in the memories of participants.

As it turns out, WOW's festivals were genuinely groundbreaking but for reasons virtually no one can any longer recall. What cannot be remembered are those crossed-dressed and sexually explicit performances that were decidedly out-of-sync with prevailing feminist sensibilities; what cannot be remembered is a preponderance of festival-goers who showed up dressed to kill, nary a Birkenstock sandal or flannel shirt among them; what cannot be remembered is the erotically charged atmosphere that permeated nearly every dimension of the festivals. What made WOW's festivals so breathtaking at the time cannot be recalled because it is counterintuitive; after all, feminists just didn't do that kind of thing back then. As we all now know, feminists in 1980 were dour and prudish; they didn't think playfully about gender or positively about sex until the 1990s with the advent of queer culture, third wave feminism, and girl (or "grrl") culture. "Memory," as Joseph Roach reminds us, "is a process that depends crucially on forgetting" (2).

The archive produced descriptions of an overwhelming number of events from both festivals representing all kinds of women's theater, music, dance, poetry, and standup comedy. Scattered among these were a few anomalies, specifically the Radical Lesbian Feminist Terrorist Comedy Group, an over-the-top sketch comedy troupe; The Flamboyant Ladies, a black lesbian theater company so provocative that one of their performances cost WOW its space; Jordy Mark's seductive evening of cabaret called Sex, Drag, and Rock 'n'

Roles, with its leather-dyke aesthetic; Pamela Camhe's moody, erotic "Lesbian Vogue" photographs of cross-dressed women with mustaches and sexy femmes presented with music in a seamless fade-in-fade-out slide show; the original production of *Split Britches* by Deb Margolin, Peggy Shaw, and Lois Weaver, a play that would be heralded as "a masterpiece of feminist theater" by 1987 (Jenkins 310); and three strippers from a working-class bar in Jersey who talked about their lives in the business while stripping for an all-women audience. These performances go a long way toward explaining why participants remember the festivals as exciting and radically different. Still, as breakers in a sea of over eighty other performances, they do not explain the charged atmosphere of the festivals in general. That is attributable in part to the festivals' rowdy, most unusual-for-the-times audiences.

The day before the first festival opened, Bethany Haye described the fund-raising events preceding it: "For those who came along to the 'Summer Nights' performances with impressions of an all-female haunt straight out of *The Killing of Sister George*, a great surprise was in store. The audiences were as boisterous and chummy as a girls' hockey team, stomping and catcalling their appreciation . . . shouting alternative punchlines to the comics' bits. Not one pair of orthopedic shoes was spotted." The flier for Mark's cabaret encouraged audience members to "attend as your drag fantasy." During a lull in the performance, spectators hit the runway for an impromptu fashion show. In an article published shortly after the festival closed, Barbara Baracks wrote, "For two-and-a-half weeks I ducked in and out of the 50 or so events going on. . . . Witches, nuns and ladies bearded in glitter kept dropping in. The performers had a hard time not being outdone by the feistiness of the audience" (23).

In retrospect, WOW's ethos resonates with what emerged in the 1990s under the compelling and productive rubric "queer." Queer signals and encompasses a wide range of identities, theories, and sensibilities, evolving in part as a reaction against the identity politics and leanings toward assimilation that characterize Stonewall-era gay and lesbian rights movements. Queer is also a reaction against particular kinds of feminism. As queer became an ever more important site for progressive art and thought, feminism came to be viewed in a peculiarly totalizing way—all feminists tended to be lumped together and branded as prudes and anti-pornography partisans by queer theorists and third-generation feminists alike. Stereotypes do not emerge from a vacuum, and the 1970s certainly produced its share of staid, humorless feminists. But it was feminists who, at the dawn of the 1980s, produced festivals that included smart, wildly funny, and erotically charged performances. The project of my book, then, would be to rediscover feminism's lost genealogy and resurrect those instances of cultural production that reverse a sleight-of-hand that made of *all* feminists "*the* feminists." Much exciting and important contemporary work is miscast as antithetical to an aesthetic history that, in fact, at the very least profoundly informs it and, I would argue, largely produced it.

The inability of those women who actually attended the festivals to re-member what was so breathtaking about them marks the beginning of a trajectory in which much is forgotten over time about work of significance and influence. "Collective memory works selectively, imaginatively, and often perversely," according to Roach, and "selective memory requires public enact-ments of forgetting, either to blur the obvious discontinuities, misalliances, and ruptures or . . . to exaggerate them in order to mystify a previous Golden Age, now lapsed" (2–3). Far from mystifying or glorifying a previous period, the inability to recall some of the festivals' most salient features is a conse-quence of maligning a previous age. Vilifying feminists as dour prudes and feminism as essentialist, assimilationist, and anti-sex had a totalizing effect; what was in fact a reaction against specific kinds of feminism effectively sealed off further consideration of other feminisms and their multiple sensibilities. "Feminists didn't do that kind of thing back then" is the resulting conviction, collectively held in cultural memory. In other words, rising up from a sea of over eighty feminist performance pieces were a handful of performances that largely account for the overwhelming sense of WOW's festivals as utterly new and unique. They can no longer be remembered, however, because a reductive, simplified version of feminist history dominates the current discourse, seal-ing off access to these anomalous performances in collective memory. Hence, a significant dimension of feminist history is lost to a process of forgetting that ultimately serves to support claims of originality for certain, sex-positive cultural developments in the 1990s. WOW's festivals belie this trajectory, providing evidence of a funny, parodic, eroticized, gender-bending aesthetic with roots firmly grounded in feminism.

While some 112 women's theaters were in existence across the United States at the time of WOW's festivals, most imploded under the strain of tensions inherent in early feminist thinking and organizational philosophies. Only a handful of women's theaters remain today, and WOW is the only one of its kind still operating in New York City. As WOW approaches nearly thirty years of uninterrupted production, it continues to reside in the East Village, where it operates as a collective in the fourth-floor walk-up space of an abandoned doll factory in a city-owned building. It functions today on an annual budget of $17,000 with no artistic director, no staff, and, until recent years, no phone. At any given moment, some thirty to thirty-five women are actively involved in WOW's collective, but hundreds have participated over time, producing some of the most significant work to emerge from Manhattan's downtown theater scene.

In the context of feminist performance from an earlier historical period, Sue-Ellen Case has written, "The traditional canon of art, literature and theatre omits almost entirely any images of lesbian experience or sexuality" (50). This was certainly true in the 1970s and 1980s as well. The desire to rectify this erasure was one of the driving forces behind the creation of the WOW Café. Similarly, a driving force behind my book became the desire to confirm the sentiments of those who contend that WOW burst on the scene as something extraordinary and then continued to surprise for over two decades. Although WOW has received much attention from feminist scholars over the years, the WOW Café Theatre and much of the significant work produced there is missing from the annals of both "legitimate theater" and avant-garde performance. WOW's accomplishment has not been fully recognized. When a phenomenon like WOW goes missing, something significant is lost not only to theater history but to cultural studies in general. When feminism goes missing, something is lost to queer.

Ten years prior to my work in the archive's Brooklyn location, I had visited the Lesbian Herstory Archives when it was the pioneering effort of Joan Nestle and housed in her apartment on the upper west side of Manhattan. The archive opened quite literally in her pantry in 1976, and by 1990, boxes, file cabinets, and piles of material were everywhere—the living room, the bedroom, the kitchen. I remember sitting on the end of Nestle's bed watching a videotape of a WOW weekly Variety Night performance on a screen only a couple of feet from my face. Nestle was particularly excited that day because she had just received the writings and photographs of lesbians of color who had defined and occupied their own subcultural space in Harlem throughout and beyond the time of the Harlem Renaissance. One of the photographs was a headshot of a strikingly beautiful, cross-dressed black woman.

Visiting this early version of the archive was emotional in ways I had not anticipated. The place was jam-packed with the evidence of so many women never written into history and long lost to memory. If women in general are absent from the historical record, lesbians are aggressively missing; for reasons of survival, their history unfolds in acts of hiding from a hostile culture. Nestle founded an archive where those who followed these women could mine the evidence of lesbian existence and bring invisible lives and untold stories to light. Nestle's crammed and cramped apartment was crushingly sonorous with silent and silenced voices—the sense of a lost people found was palpable.

The lesson I learned as an archaeologist in the lesbian archive is the crucial significance of creating and maintaining evidence of the lives and work of dominant culture's marginalized groups. In the absence of such preservation, WOW's history and its importance to an understanding of feminist history is but one example of what would be lost to the historical record. The lessons learned in the Lesbian Herstory Archives changed the direction of my book project in ways I could not have anticipated. Other lessons await discovery there.

Works Cited

Baracks, Barbara. "Witches, Nuns, and Bearded Ladies." *Soho Weekly News*, Oct. 29, 1980: 23.

Carr, C. Interview. New York. Mar. 29, 2001.

Case, Sue-Ellen. *Feminism and Theatre*. New York: Methuen, 1988.

———, ed. *Split Britches: Lesbian Practice/Feminist Performance*. London: Routledge, 1996.

The Five Lesbian Brothers (Theatre Troup). *The Five Lesbian Brothers: Four Plays*. New York: Theatre Communications Group, 2000.

Hart, Lynda, ed. *Of All the Nerve: Deb Margolin Solo*. New York: Cassell, 1999.

Haye, Bethany. "Performance." *Soho Weekly News*, Oct. 1, 1980.

Hughes, Holly. *Clit Notes: A Sapphic Sampler*. New York: Grove, 1996.

Jenkins, Linda Walsh. "Split Britches." *Women in American Theatre*. Ed. Helen Krich Chinoy and Linda Walsh Jenkins. Rev. ed. New York: Theatre Communications Group, 1987. 310–14.

Margolin, Deb. Interview. New York. June 6, 2001.

Roach, Joseph. *Cities of the Dead: Circum-Atlantic Performance*. New York: Columbia UP, 1996.

Solomon, Alisa. "The Wings of Desire: WOW Café Celebrates 20 Years of Lesbian Performance." *Village Voice*, Jan. 3–9, 2001: 61.

Troyano, Alina. *I, Carmelita Tropicana: Performing between Cultures*. Boston: Beacon, 2000.

Weaver, Lois. "Afterword. " *The Routledge Reader in Gender and Performance*. Ed. Lizbeth Goodman. London: Routledge, 1998. 303–4.

Part Four

When the Lives of
Our Research Subjects
Parallel Our Own

14

"I See Dead People"
Archive, Crypt, and an Argument for the Researcher's Sixth Sense

Elizabeth (Betsy) Birmingham

In M. Night Shyamalan's 1999 movie *The Sixth Sense*, the child-protagonist, Cole Sear, communicates—against his will and with some horror—with spirits of the dead. The movie's plot becomes increasingly complex when the child whispers to his psychologist, Malcolm Crowe, that the spirits "don't know they're dead." They don't haunt us, it seems, out of malevolence; they don't even know they haunt. My experience of research as a lived experience has involved inhabiting the cool archival spaces occupied by spirits, listening to their stories whispered in historical traces, and having them not just tolerate my presence but befriend me and shape my research.

Architect Marion Mahony Griffin (1871–1961) doesn't know that she is dead. And then again, perhaps she is not—she's quite hot right now, though I hardly know what she would think of that. The first monograph devoted solely to her work, *Marion Mahony: Drawing the Form of Nature*, was published in 2005; she had her first solo exhibition (at Northwestern's Block Museum, on the shore of Lake Michigan, near where she grew up in Winnetka, Illinois); and I recently opened the *Chronicle of Higher Education* to see her architectural work splashing the whole of the back page. Since 2005, my own published research is a tiny fraction of the scholarly activity surrounding Mahony Griffin's life and work: the Art Institute of Chicago has gone live with a beautiful Web version of her manuscript "The Magic of America"; a well-known Australian biographer has a book project under contract; and Australian and American scholars have begun the early work on a collaborative project concerning transdisciplinary approaches to understanding the cultural impact of Mahony Griffin's work. She is hot.

It is difficult to say a woman like that is dead, as she helps me shape my tenure case, write this article, teach my graduate research methods class, and secure funding to work with others, for whom she is equally alive, in Australia. As scholars who work with historical figures, we always know that we owe those figures some sort of debt, as we mine their lives (and deaths) to build our careers. But sometimes, when we are very lucky, we see dead people—people whose will won't be ignored—the relationship becomes reciprocal, and the work we do together leads to friendship and collaboration. That is the story that I have to tell.

I first learned of Marion Mahony Griffin in 1989 through my interest in her husband, Walter Burley Griffin, who was, at that time, the object of my intellectual longing. He was a turn-of-the-century architect possessed of the clean-shaven, Hollywood good looks not common during that mustached, mutton-chopped historical moment. I wrote my undergraduate honors thesis (for my art history degree) on his midwestern architecture, visiting nearly all of the thirty-some buildings still standing that he had designed between 1902 and 1913. My work was the traditional work of an architectural historian: I was studying a body of work, this group of buildings; attempting to determine contemporary addresses for each; using building records, city phone books, and architectural magazines to accurately date the buildings; and upon developing an accurate chronology, making some claims about the aesthetic development of the architect.

Because I was an undergraduate, much of this work really had been done some years before; there existed a solid history of secondary scholarship on the subject of Walter Burley Griffin's architecture extending back to 1964, including several references from the 1950s. Nonetheless, I undertook my charge diligently, revisiting the primary sources: I visited the Cook County records office and the Chicago Historical Society and dug through hundreds of mildewed issues of *Construction News* and *Western Architect* and ancient telephone books. My goal, as I understood it, was to suggest that Griffin's architectural skills developed in a way that made his work diverge from that of his mentor, Frank Lloyd Wright. I compiled note cards, created chronologies, and tried to understand what happened after 1910–11 that so changed his architectural style that he moved from being a follower of Wright to being an innovator in his own right.

I never met Mahony Griffin in these places, nor in the secondary scholarship written about her husband as I absorbed that scholarship unquestioningly. I knew that Walter married, at thirty-four, a woman six years older, who was, as a contemporary wrote, "Frank Lloyd Wright's most talented assistant." I found traces of her, though much of the information in secondary sources was contradictory (or wrong): her name was usually misspelled (Marian, or Mahoney, or both); her dates of birth, death, graduation, and marriage varied by source. Although many sources mention both Griffins and even include Mahony Griffin in their indices, she receives mention only because

of her marriage to Walter. She is characterized as a pupil, a wife, and a draftsman—but not as a highly educated and competent architect in her own right.
In all the secondary scholarship I read, written from 1947 to 1989, that one
piece of information remained consistent. Though she may have designed a
few buildings, though she graduated from MIT with a degree in architecture,
though she was the first woman in the country licensed to practice architecture, she wasn't really an architect. She was a "draftsman," something lesser
and dismissible. And I believed it, dismissing her. Those telling me so were
scholars, scholars whose published credibility was intoxicating to me because
I wanted to be one of them.

I first met Mahony Griffin herself through her 1,000-page manuscript,
"The Magic of America," housed in the Burnham Library of Chicago's Art
Institute. As an undergraduate in 1989, I carried to the archive a note from
my art history professor, who had arranged this meeting, who had vouched
for my integrity. I sat in the fluorescent archives, wearing white cotton gloves,
leafing through Mahony Griffin's musty typescript, breathing her in, unable
to read more than bits in the two days I had allowed for my research. Her
typescript was a baffling puzzle of things—at my first glance perhaps more
a huge scrapbook than a manuscript. It hid more of her than it revealed to
me, a labyrinthine catacomb of stuff never quite catalogued or described by
an archivist, just artifacts arranged by Mahony Griffin herself: architectural
drawings, newspaper clippings, postcards, letters, lists of the native plants of
Australia, texts of speeches delivered by her and by Walter—all wrapped a
strange story of the entwined lives of two architects, lives that she described
as a series of four "battles." I found both an unreadable text and a text that
haunted me—by the time I left, I was convinced that the text, described in the
card catalogue only as "a biography of architect Walter Burley Griffin," was
something other than that. My note cards and chronologies helped me piece
together a story of parallel paths that suddenly crossed, leading to architectural
work such as neither had previously produced: the 1912 winning design for
the international competition to build an entire city, the Australian national
capital at Canberra.

Yet nothing that I had read in the secondary scholarship I obsessively
consumed had described the text, or Mahony Griffin herself, in any but the
most dismissive terms. The top scholars in my field described her variously
as "coldly intellectual" (Birrell 14), "bitter and critical" (132), and lacking
"the imaginative mind to create" (Brooks 164). Her work was easily labeled
"derivative" (Van Zanten 21), and her architecture was "inconsistent, lacked
restraint, and was not architecturally rationalized" (Johnson 12). Her text
was dismissed much more thoroughly by scholars as the ranting of a senile

and bitter old woman. These traces, the only discussion of her available to me through secondary sources in 1989, worked to erase any interpretation of her life or work as interesting or important. It is not surprising that I became certain that my engagement with and interest in the text and its author suggested something lax about my scholarship—a lack of discernment that would mark me naive and unsophisticated. Although "The Magic of America" was the richest document I found in my research, and my guesses about it were the only original conclusions that came from my research, I did not mention or cite the text in my undergraduate thesis, perhaps out of fear that my interest in a thing so dismissible would reveal that I really wasn't a scholar, that I was easily sidetracked by the unimportant. So I became possessed by a secret, a secret whispered by a text, written by a dead women, misidentified by archivists, ignored by scholars. The text was not a biography of one architect but an autobiography of a joined career and a collaboration, two lives, and a shared love for architecture.

Architectural theorist Mark Wigley, citing Jacques Derrida, suggests that the crypt is the secret itself, formed by the not telling, "the act of vomiting to the inside" constructed of the tension of the "internal resistance of the vault like pillars, beams, studs, and retaining walls, leaning the powers of intolerable pain against an ineffable, forbidden pleasure" (qtd. in Bloomer 155). The pain was the haunting knowledge that in order to become an architectural historian, I had to give up the work I found interesting, the excavation of texts for those minute traces that documented the contributions of people long dead, long dismissed, and thoroughly discredited. The pleasure was of being possessed of and by a secret knowledge—evidence, clear evidence, I thought, that joined fortunes led two architects to produce better work than either had been capable of alone. When I hinted at this knowledge, later, while in my architectural history master's program, a professor, a very smart professor, suggested that to tell such secrets would be "academic suicide." Historians never speculate, he offered. I am not the first student to have felt this tension among secret, crypt, pain, and pleasure, a tension that I would now identify as "discipline." But at the time, I knew only that when faced with a difference between what published scholars knew and what I guessed, I had to follow published scholars—that is how "we" build knowledge, and to do otherwise is "suicide."

More than fifteen years later, I still cringe at the real secret: that I so wanted to be an architectural historian that I refused to tell the story I was beginning to understand, that my note cards and chronologies did add up to something—an intellectual collaboration that enabled these two minor architects to produce work that would win an international competition. Discipline instead required me to tell a sideways story that maintained the fragile architecture of those histories I knew, the ones that described a male genius and a talented assistant whose skill as an artist helped her husband become successful. When I wrote about Mahony Griffin in 1991, in my aborted attempt to finish my master's degree in architectural studies, I even spelled her name Mahoney, as had the scholars I cited, even though I had seen her name, Mahony, typed by her own hand on the title page of her typescript when I read it in the archive.

This is my secret. I did not simply succumb to some perceived disciplinary pressure (I did that when I agreed to write about her husband's architectural work rather than about her text as my master's thesis). I talked myself into believing (with the help of the many scholars who claimed it) that perhaps Mahony Griffin herself had been senile, or perverse, or mistaken about many things. About the spelling of her own name? The weight of discipline made it seem more reasonable that she be mistaken about the spelling of her own name than that many scholars, one of whom sat on my thesis committee, could all be wrong. Mistaken.

If historians don't even speculate, I assumed they also did not misspell. I still struggle to understand who I was that I could have been made to doubt so easily. As a scholar, I had to make up an implausible story so that I could be wrong in good company. My discipline itself kept me distanced from the subject of my research, but not so that I might objectively evaluate the information I had collected. Rather, my discipline sought to narrow potential interpretations and to enforce, rigidly, the notion that my work must build on that of other scholars—even those who were mistaken—and that any other interpretation was speculation. And my professors, who walked me through this process, were smart and generous and careful scholars, as were the scholars whose work I was reading and parroting and internalizing and rebelling against, and I wanted to be like them. And I couldn't.

I wish I could say that Marion compelled me, or enabled me, or inspired me, or haunted me until I abandoned my dysfunctional relationship with my first academic love, architectural history. And perhaps she did, but mostly I just left, not for her but for me, abandoning a degree into which I had invested thousands of dollars and hundreds of hours of research. When I tried to explain to my thesis director, I could only say, "I can't do this. I think it's methodological." And perhaps it always is, but I think that I just didn't see *her*—I saw only the person that my disciplined vision allowed me to see.

If I met Marion Mahony in 1989, I befriended her in 1999, after I became a rhetorician (and no longer worried about being in the good company of architectural historians) and felt empowered to tell, finally, the most interesting story I knew. For the first time, I sat with her text. In that same fluorescent archive, she emerged as I read her letters. I read them as if they had been written to me, as if she were entrusting me with her story, her life, her love, and her career. I sat and cried. She wrote of falling in love at forty:

> But when I encountered W.B.G. I was swept off my feet by my delight in his achievements in my profession, then through the common bond of interests in nature and intellectual pursuits and then with the man himself. It was by no means a case of love at first sight, but it was a madness when it struck. ("Magic of America" IV 157)

But it was her letter to Walter's sister and brother-in-law describing her presence at Walter's death, so far from home together in India in 1937, that caused my crying:

> Then as his breath began to fail, I talked to him, told him what a wonderful life I had had with him, how he was beloved by everybody and suddenly he turned and fastened his eyes wide open and round on mine, startled and intense as if it had never occurred to him that he could die and they never left mine till he ceased breathing and I closed them. (I 305)

She never forgave Walter for dying too young, for leaving her alone for so many years. She never had another design built. There is no question that for nearly ten years, I had had a professional relationship with this talented woman—a relationship that had allowed me to study her life and puzzle about her work. Why then, on that day, did I first see her? What was it that made me cry, that made her befriend me?

The researcher's sixth sense isn't the ability to see the dead but our potential to help the dead, who do not know they are dead, finish their stories, and we do this in the moment in which we realize that their stories are ours. For many years, I found myself frustrated by those scholarly representations that subsumed Mahony Griffin's architectural work within that of her husband's, those representations that refused to describe a collaborative, mutually nourishing relationship at the heart of an exceptionally creative architectural practice. Is this the story that keeps me awake at night? The story my fellow scholars have told that seems most deeply false, mean-spirited, and unjust to my friend? No, not even close.

It has taken me more than fifteen years to understand the promise that has grown from my friendship with a woman who died before I was born. That promise, which has become my responsibility as a researcher, has led to my interest not in teasing apart some truth of her life, not in seeing it as a life that needs me to ride in like the cavalry to recover its importance, but to ask why it is a life that should need recovering at all. Mahony Griffin's is a well-documented life. There are buildings, publications, letters, treatises, postcards, architectural drawings, blueprints, manifestos; a 1,000-page autobiography; mentions of her work by contemporaries, in manuscript memoirs, and in varied publications; records of her birth, her death, her college graduation, her senior thesis, her career as a professional, her passion for the theater, her public speeches, and her parties. These exist, with her name always correctly spelled, pages and pages and pages of primary records, nearly all unconsulted—in fact, nearly all dismissed—by a generation of highly trained scholars and historians who have in turn been almost exclusively consulted by a second generation of highly trained scholars and historians.

I became a rhetorician, and not a historian, so that my research could span the questions imposed by discipline. My research shifted from the attempt to pin down architectural influences, chronologies, and construction histories to attempting to pin down scholars—to examine our questions, our methods, and our preoccupations—noting the things we value and how those values shape the knowledge they claim to benignly reflect. My promise to my friend Marion has been to make visible the ways in which the language of architectural history has shaped her rich life into one that is dismissible, and has done so despite shelves of evidence to the contrary. And this was done so easily, and nearly accidentally and without malice, to a woman who did everything within her power to document the life she wanted remembered, a woman whose signature is everywhere and whose marks and traces cover three continents and shape major cities. If this can happen to her, not because of some grand conspiracy or international scholarly plot but rather because of uninterrogated habits of scholarship ingrained in us through an education of strict discipline, should it surprise us that we know so little of so few women in art, architecture, music, science, engineering? My argument for the researcher's sixth sense is not that it will enable us to recover and converse with the lost dead, to understand them in a way that is definitive and true, but that they will help us recover ourselves, help us discover that we did not know that we were the dead, inhabiting the crypt, repeating dead histories in dead languages.

Works Cited

Biemiller, Lawrence. "The Artist behind the Architect." *Chronicle of Higher Education*, Dec. 2, 2005.

Birrell, James. *Walter Burley Griffin*. Brisbane: U of Queensland P, 1964.

Bloomer, Jennifer. *Architecture and the Text: The (S)crypts of Joyce and Piranesi*. New Haven: Yale UP, 1993.

Brooks, H. Allen. *The Prairie School: Frank Lloyd Wright and His Midwest Contemporaries*. New York: Norton, 1972.

Griffin, Marion Mahony. "The Magic of America." Unpublished typescript. New-York Historical Society, c. 1949.

Johnson, Donald Leslie. *The Architecture of Walter Burley Griffin*. Melbourne: Macmillan Co. of Australia, 1977.

Van Zanten, David. "The Early Work of Marion Mahony Griffin." *Prairie School Review* 3.2 (1969): 5–23.

Wood, Debora, ed. *Marion Mahony Griffin: Drawing the Form of Nature*. Evanston: Northwestern UP, 2005.

15

Stitching and Writing a Life
Liz Rohan

I found my research subject Janette Miller (1879–1969), a librarian, diarist, missionary, preacher, and poet, and she "found" me about fifteen years ago at the University of Michigan's Bentley Historical Library. A senior at the university, I was researching the diaries of a man who had owned a home in Ann Arbor that I was studying for an architecture project. After a cursory glance at the man's diaries, I knew I would find nothing about his house from them. But it got me curious about the library's other diaries. I zeroed in on the description in the finding aide for Janette's diaries: "Interesting in a personal way. Some dream entries." Her writing (about a dozen leather-bound diaries plus her correspondence and photograph collection from her work as a missionary) is stored at this library. Janette's brother's family donated the material to the library in the 1970s. In 1990, I had been the first to study them.

Intrigued, I returned to read these diaries when I had time a few months later and spent several days combing over them. Seven years afterward, I decided I wanted to write about Janette's work and went back to read her diaries many times thereafter while also combing over the items documenting her sixty-year career as a missionary in Angola. Her writing first inspired me to pursue my Ph.D., eventually became the topic of my dissertation, and is now the topic of my current book project. The process I have gone through to gain intimacy with these texts, and by default with Janette Miller the person, has coaxed me into academe, arguably directed my career thus far in it, and—overall—has helped me to solidify a method for understanding texts and the lives invariably shaping them. Part of the research method I outline here shows the benefits of research beyond the obvious; the archives Janette Miller left behind not only inspired my research methods but helped me mature as a person and scholar.

Janette began writing in her diaries when she was about fourteen, in 1893, and stopped writing in them when she left the United States for Angola when she was thirty, in 1909. At first, she was more inclined to write about the details of her life and used blank-book diaries. This attention to extensive narrative tapered off over the years as she used her diary more as a combination accounting ledger, photo album, and scrapbook. She also began the habit of pasting in copies of letters she had sent and received into the pages of her diaries.

Even though almost seven years had elapsed between my first and second visit to Janette's diaries, I remained tied to her life and writing. Keeping a diary was important to Janette, as it had been to me; like her, I began writing in a diary when I was a teenager. Although I had read published diaries before, in 1990 Janette's diaries were the first and only ones I had thus far seen "in the flesh." Also, Janette was a prolific dreamer and recorded her dreams in her diaries; I too use my diaries to record my dreams. Thus, I felt bonded to Janette due to our shared literate activities. Moreover, in the seven years I stayed "away" from Janette, I never forgot this quotation she copied into the back of her diary for 1903 that I read the first time I found the diaries:

Guidelines for Christian Living

Find out what God is doing, [do] not initiate our own work and when he requires our presence for his own plans use (1) Bible (2) Pure motives (3) Surrender will (4) Use reason (5) Much prayer (6) Ask for all other doors be closed (7) Watch for circumstance (8) *Try not to be guided by the whole plan, but the next stitch.* We often make the mistake thinking that God is not guiding us at all because we cannot see far ahead. But this is not his method. He only undertakes that the steps of a good man be ordered by the Lord. (emphasis mine)

She wrote underneath them, "Grandma tells of minister who said, 'God doesn't give *dying* grace to *live* by.'"

As I graduated from college and embarked upon my journey into the real world, to work in Chicago (two months after reading Janette's diaries for the first time), these "directions" from Janette's diary remained inspirational, if implicitly. In my diary, I adopted the metaphor of the "stitch." The idea of *living* as a process and an ever-evolving plan paralleled for me the act of writing life experiences into a diary or journal. As a diary writer, I had learned to look at my life as an evolving story of disparate details that eventually come together, upon reflection, to make a whole. And then, faced with new obstacles and questions, the cycle would begin again. Also, as I studied Janette's writing, our narratives became synthesized (or stitched together) as I shared some of her experiences.

Later, when I looked through Janette's diaries again, I ascertained that she had gotten this quotation from her grandmother during the summer of 1903, when Janette had visited with her for a time. Her grandmother was a devout woman who struggled with her faith. During an intimate moment with her grandmother that summer, Janette probably accessed these Christian Living guidelines, which she copied into the Memorandum section of her 1903 diary, next to directions for eliminating "falling hair."

When I read Janette's diaries in college, and when I found the Christian Living guidelines, I was primarily interested in her dreams (the sleeping kind). She wrote vividly of one dream in particular. When she was seventeen, she had a nightmare that a wedding (in which she was the bride) took a foreboding turn when her mother and the groom failed to show up for it. Five years later, practically to the date of this dream, in 1902, Janette's mother, Cora, died. Janette wrote often during her mother's illness, scribbling Bible verses at the top of the pages of her diary. Cora lay bedridden for a year, suffering frequent convulsions; her death was slow and painful. Janette became very close to her mother when working as her caretaker and also trying to attend school and work part-time.

When I went back to read the diaries seven years later, I visited them in Ann Arbor on the way to spend time with my parents in their Detroit-area home where I grew up. Learning more about Janette, I became interested in why she chose to become a missionary, which, I'd learn, linked her dreams (but for the future) to larger historical trends. Armed with this question after a long January afternoon at the Bentley Historical Library with Janette's 1908 diary, I found a telling paragraph alluding to her frustration with her life as a librarian and her choice to become a missionary, what she called "special service for the master." When I better understood Janette's method for meaning-making in her diary, I realized that this paragraph was from a letter she had sent to her former high school teacher Miss Hull, who was also a mentor and friend:

> I cannot stand another year of irresolution and miserable sense of failure. Better attempt something with hope and courage than stand irresolute on the brink, or settle back to give up. . . . This thought of beginning life again at age 30 does not daunt me, but to live life useless fills me with terror. There has been an undercurrent of deep dissatisfaction this year with merely working to earn a living and living to earn my bread. Library work is interesting and pleasant and educational—as delightful work as I could find, it is not doing any special service for the master. I promised to serve . . . so I ought to have every day work which would be service.

I had just turned twenty-nine years old when I read this passage, and I appreciated the courage it would have taken to leave friends and family for the unknown, "beginning life again at age 30." This paragraph was the "next stitch" for me to consider as I left Janette's work again.

When I at last sat down with the notes I had taken from Janette's diaries, hoping to create an article about them, I decided to structure the piece by attempting to find out why Janette might have become frustrated with her life as a librarian and why she was inspired to become a missionary. As I researched the historical period when Janette wrote in her diaries—from 1893 to 1909—I was also reconsidering my plan to get a Ph.D. in composition and rhetoric (a plan I had abandoned the year previously). My first official writing about Janette was in my personal statements to graduate schools. I wrote that Janette's decision to begin her life over at thirty was giving me the courage to do the same.

On top of this "stitch" attaching me to Janette, I was also experiencing some of her frustrations. Like her, I did not have time to dedicate myself to the work that made me feel good about myself professionally or vocationally. During the time I was writing about her, I was working three jobs, not only to make ends meet and to pay off debts but to feel satisfied. While I held a mentally taxing but financially unrewarding job in the writing center of a high school, where I was also the debate coach, I was additionally teaching a writing class at night. The only time I could get to a library to do research was after school, when I was tired. Because I was no longer a student at any of the Chicago-area university libraries I visited, I couldn't check out books. I had to make it to the Northwestern University Library before five o'clock, when "visitors" were no longer admitted. My motivation to write about Janette's life without the time or the resources to do so helped me to understand her even more. I too had become too busy "earning my bread" to dedicate myself to what I loved: writing and scholarship. My day job held me back from doing my "work." Like Janette, I needed to go for it—leave my secure life in Chicago for my Ph.D. in another city, which I did the following year. The "directions" for my life had been buried in Janette's diary for years. Yet until I was ready to read them, they weren't mine to find.

In her reflections about her relationship to women's rhetoric and the methodology she adopts when writing about female rhetoricians, contributor Christine Mason Sutherland recalls her Oxford college teachers who encouraged her to respond to primary texts with the naïveté of what might be considered a gut reaction. Secondary sources were to be consulted only after an impression had been made about the primary source of interest (111). I initially discovered Janette's writing—her diaries composed as a young girl and young woman—with this so-called naive approach. I was simply interested in diaries, and in primary sources, as a college senior. I hadn't an agenda or an academic career. Perhaps unconsciously, as I returned to Janette's texts as a burgeoning scholar and as I decided to write about life and texts for my Ph.D. dissertation, I recalled the value of a so-called naive reaction to another woman's life and materials outlining them, the value of "watch[ing] for circumstance[s]," honoring the stitch over a plan. I was implicitly dedicated to the analytical approach I had adopted at the onset of my discovery of Janette's texts. I was to resist critique; I was to wait for the "next stitch" each time I brought new clues and contexts to my research tasks. This was especially important when I began to write about and research Janette's lifetime project as missionary. I could relate to her diary texts set in modern institutions in the relatively familiar environs of the turn-of-the-twentieth-century Midwestern cities where Janette had spent her childhood and young womanhood—Chicago, Omaha, and later Detroit. But when Janette—whose focus was on converting others to Christianity—moved out of her diary to Angola, where she lived and worked in a colonial context as a missionary for sixty years, my project and burgeoning affinity with Janette as a subject became more complicated if strained.

Although alienated by her evangelical impulses, I also noticed that when I engaged with Janette's texts, my life became better as I became less judgmental of others. For the most part, the colonial context in which Janette wrote made me conscious about any colonizing moves on my part as a researcher. Most significantly, the challenge of following a stitch and foregoing an understanding of a pattern, or rather imposing a pattern onto data, was made comprehensive for me by my several trips to find the house where Janette lived in the early 1900s, on Avery Street in Detroit. The journey was technically tangential to my research. But I was fairly certain that 221 Avery, a historic, architectural, and geographic text, was a profoundly important site for Janette. This was where Janette had nursed her very ill mother for a year and from where her father had hastily moved the family immediately after Cora's death.

Thus, my trip to Avery Street was a kind of pilgrimage to a sacred place in Janette's life, a kind of nostalgic and reverent errand I did initially "for her." Just as the paragraph Janette wrote when she was thirty about her choice to be a missionary inspired me to get my Ph.D., Janette's other private texts promoted action on my part. I was inspired to embark upon this trip when seeing that on a list of the deaths of her family members in her scrapbook, Janette had jotted "221 Avery" next to the date of her mother's death. Although I have still not located the exact house in which the Millers lived in 1903 because the address on the house has changed, during my trips through Detroit to look for this house, I confronted my own emotional relationship to the space where Janette once lived—a now socio-economically depressed Detroit whose many inhabitants are black and poor. My obvious task, according to standard academic practice, necessitated an interrogation of Janette's subjectivity as a white middle-class woman working in a politicized situation, in Africa "converting natives." However, my recursive trips to find Janette's former home resulted in revelations to my own self about my subjectivity as a white middle-class woman who grew up in the racially polarized space of Metro-Detroit. My trip was at first designed for Janette, the stitch, but then I realized that the trips benefited me, a greater plan.

The Detroit landscape, a research site obviously outside of the archives, also helped me to understand Janette's subjectivity. When exploring the multiracial Detroit neighborhood of Woodbridge where Janette had once lived on Avery, whereupon I met its racially diverse twenty-first-century habitants who tried to help me find 221 Avery, I discovered a more complex racial script than the one I had been taught to imagine growing up. Janette Miller's story indeed depicts a complicated script when it comes to racial politics. At the end of her life, she was running a mission, the Ebenezer Orphanage, with the help of a biracial, transnational administration. One of her partners was a Portuguese woman, the other an African woman. My trips through Detroit to visit 221 Avery made me think about and value Janette's experience; my trips urged me not to simplify her situation.

These trips through Detroit also led me to new data and further showcase the serendipitous discoveries of the research process described by others in this volume. After I had visited Avery Street one June day, I decided to learn more about historical Detroit at the Detroit Public Library. In old city phone directories, I looked up all the Millers who lived in the city in 1905. Though I didn't necessarily need this information for my write-up about Janette's diaries, it was thrilling to see that these ordinary texts, the phone books, corroborated what I had learned from Janette's diaries. The phone books indicated that in 1905, Janette had lived with her brother Frank and near her aunt Kate, whom I had come to know in the diaries. My curiosity and desultory approach to archival work paid off that day when I impulsively looked in the card catalogue for anything by or about Janette Miller and discovered that she had apparently donated a textbook to the library that she had written in the African language Umbundu, entitled *Ortografia*. Published in 1921, it is an important artifact for me in reconstructing Janette's experience as a missionary, which I continue to investigate. The methodological approach that helped me to find Janette Miller's papers in the first place—vague curiosity—led me to new clues for "piecing" the story of her life together.

The process I undertook while building major projects from the data I found so long ago when a young and novice undergraduate scholar reinforces an adage I learned from a senior scholar when in graduate school and just beginning my dissertation: "The work will show you how to do it." One obvious plan that manifested from "piecing together" Janette's story with her texts: it prepared me for the surprising conclusion to my search for an academic job. One of my three job offers was at the University of Michigan–Dearborn,

located in the Detroit suburbs, which I took. My spiritual and physical recon-
nection with the Detroit area prepared me for a more intense homecoming,
a real and hopefully permanent one. My research about Janette prepared me
spiritually for this circumstance—it showed me how to get home and, more
than anything, made me appreciate this home. More logically, I was aided
by the project materially because the research provided me the ethos and the
degree to land the job.

The recursive process of leaving home and coming home that I confronted
when writing about Janette parallels also a function of women's diary writing,
noted by Suzanne Bunkers and Cynthia Huff, which they read as a sustained,
if cyclical, attempt by the diarist "self" to assess and renew her commitment to
others (19). Diarists continue through time, writing over time, but constantly
return home to a physical location—the diary itself. Following the stitch, as
a diarist and a student of diaries, has thus far not surprisingly led me on a
circuitous and rewarding journey. My encounter with Janette's story shaped
my methods for making meaning not only of her life but of other texts and
lives that I have encountered through other research projects—including, of
course, my own.

Works Cited

Bunkers, Suzanne, and Cynthia A. Huff. "Issues in Women's Diaries: A
    Theoretical and Critical Introduction." *Inscribing the Daily: Critical Essays
    on Women's Diaries*. Ed. Suzanne Bunkers and Cynthia A. Huff. Amherst:
    U of Massachusetts P, 1996. 1–20.
Miller, Janette. Papers of Janette Miller, Congregationalist Missionary to
    Angola, box 1. Bentley Historical Library, U of Michigan, Ann Arbor.
Sutherland, Christine Mason. "Feminist Historiography: Research Methods
    in Rhetoric." *Rhetoric Society Quarterly* (Winter 2002): 109–22.

16

When Two Stories Collide, They Catch Fire

Anca Vlasopolos

I go back to the summer of 2001. Inveterate insomniac that I am, I must have dozed off because I awake clutching the sheet so tightly my knuckles are frozen in fists, and it hurts when I unfurl my hands. A disreputable old sailor in patchwork clothes has just handed me a sack. He's pleased with himself and with me, his grin crinkling up his dry-leather face and showing gums. It's a gift, from the heart, he says, spit flying from his mouth. What have I done to earn it? I open it. No pearls—a cascade of whole and broken shells and sand pours out. A dried blowfish. A very old piece of salt cod on its way to fossil. And, last, a bird's corpse. I recognize it instantly—the golden head, downy breast, black-barred wing tips and tail: a short-tailed albatross. The old man winks. He says, "I know you're interested in these. I shot one for you." (Vlasopolos)

In 2001, there were only fourteen hundred of these birds alive in the world. Each summer, a few die unnatural deaths as they get tangled up in long lines of fishing vessels and then drown.

How did it begin, this interest leading to the nightmare? The first story began on Cape Cod. Along Route 28 one summer, my great friend Joseph Prescott, formerly my professor, then my colleague, told me a charming story. True intellectual, he made it a point to visit whatever university or college happened to be in any town where he paused on his travels—or if not a university or college, at least the public library.

In Fairhaven, Massachusetts, Joe said, there's a public library with a huge glass case displaying a kimono, a samurai sword, and other Japanese artifacts. Intrigued, Joe asked the librarian about the origin of this display, and he was treated to an unusual bit of local history: in the 1840s, a Japanese boy was rescued from a deserted island in the Pacific by a whaling ship, whose captain took to the boy, brought him to Fairhaven, educated him, and helped him make his way back to Japan. The boy, named Manjiro, became the first professor of English at what was later to become Tokyo University. Joe and I, professors of English, each first in our families to make a home in English, thought it an apt instance of life's surprises. At the time, I thought it a bit of local color and quickly abandoned it to some corner of my mind.

Several years later, the international issue of *National Wildlife Magazine* carried a story about the short-tailed, or Steller's, albatross, one of those half-empty, half-full tales of extinction's brink (Steiner). The story told by Rick Steiner arrived via Hiroshi Hasegawa, the world's authority on the short-tailed albatross, and involves Manjiro Nakahama, a nineteenth-century world traveler—the very same, it turns out, as the boy who grew to manhood in Fairhaven. The short-tailed albatross, the bird presented to me in my nightmare, is the largest and reputedly most beautiful albatross of the Pacific; it nests primarily on a volcanic island, Torishima (Bird Island), off the coast of Japan. Sometime after 1863, Steiner recounts, Manjiro (who by now as a samurai was allowed to choose a last name—Nakahama, based on his birthplace) went on a whaling mission for the Japanese government; he told an acquaintance, Nakaemon Tamaoiki, of the unbridled appetite for exotic feathers in the West. Manjiro's knowledge about industrial-scale exploitation of animals had been acquired during his sojourn in the United States after his rescue from Torishima by an American whaling ship. As I read these paragraphs describing the rescued and repatriated Japanese and his role in the eventual demise of the albatross, my heart started pounding. Joe's story—of the saved boy educated in Fairhaven and then returned to Japan—stirred, broke through the dust and filaments of disuse, and galvanized me. I read on . . .

Manjiro's acquaintance Tamaoiki took Manjiro's advice and set up a feather-and-skin factory on Torishima.[1] The workers decimated the albatross population as they processed the long feathers for fashion export and the pure down for stuffing thousands of quilts and pillows. From the clouds of birds, estimated at about five million, that livened the skies and linked through flight California, Alaska, Japan, and even China, only three thousand remained by 1932. The human population of "harvesters" did not fare well, either. In 1902, a volcanic eruption buried the entire village, killing all 129 inhabitants. But by then the albatross had become famous enough as sources of revenue, and another colony of hunters came to make a life of death.

In 1932, the Japanese government, influenced, after decades, by the international conservation impetus that had led to the formation of preservationist societies such as the Audubon, recognized the value of the short-tailed albatross and decided to make Torishima a sanctuary to protect the birds. However, the impoverished men on the island, still eking out a living from the few remaining birds, became enraged and proceeded to kill all the albatross that were left, so as to make a last profit from them. Not for nothing are albatross called goonies, boobies, *ahodori*—fool birds. After centuries of misuse by humans, they still think they belong. They cling tenaciously to their nesting grounds and refuse to be frightened into flight. As if the loving and vengeful spirit of Coleridge's poem watched over the slaughter, the volcano erupted again in 1939, burying the settlements; the humans this time were rescued. The island became, as Manjiro had known it, desolate for humans, for a time.

During World War II, a garrison was stationed on Torishima. After the war, in 1947, when a new meteorological station was built, a meteorologist who climbed the height of the volcanic cliffs saw large birds with white breasts; he counted three albatross. Yet the species was declared extinct in 1949, when an expedition from the Audubon Society circled Torishima and saw no trace of the birds. In 1951, ten albatross were sighted. These were descendants of thirty juveniles who had taken to sea for their three years of wandering the oceans, without alighting on land, before returning to nest where they were born; they had thus escaped the carnage of the 1930s. In 1951, Japan began protecting the short-tailed albatross. In 1962, they were declared a national monument.

From 1976 to the present, the man responsible for the precarious and still uncertain survival of this species is Hiroshi Hasegawa, a Japanese ornithologist at Toho University, recognized universally as the guardian of the short-tailed albatross.[2] That I would meet Dr. Hasegawa, that he would befriend me and be my guide through the complicated research I eventually undertook, part of it in a country whose language I do not know, was not something I would have been able to predict from that fortuitous first connection between my friend's story, woven to entertain during a seaside drive, and Rick Steiner's moving essay, in which the returning, U.S.-acculturated Manjiro brought with him more than a knowledge of English—he brought the knowledge of the profits to be made from killing wild animals. During the year following the serendipitous conjunction of the two narratives regarding Manjiro, I was also working on a new course on animal rights and wrongs. I did extensive research on the industrial-scale hunting of whales and birds in the nineteenth century, and the life of Manjiro seemed a natural thread to follow toward my sense that globalization entails unforeseen dangers as well as the often-touted benefits. I began the research for what became my historical novel.

Early in the composition, I decided that I needed to travel to an island where albatross abound, in the way that they used to crowd the slopes of Torishima before the island even had a name. I wanted to experience for myself what Manjiro had felt, amid birds in the millions—the sounds, the smell, the movement. The only albatross island to which I could travel without special permission was Midway Island, which has a very healthy population of both Laysan and black-footed albatross. I was ready to make reservations for the trip, but, to ensure that I would be on Midway at the right season, when the birds nest, and that I would be allowed to walk among them, I wrote Beth Flint, U.S. Fish and Wildlife Refuge manager for Midway, about my plans. She replied that if I wanted to see the short-tailed albatross, I should get in touch with Hiroshi Hasegawa in Japan. She kindly included his e-mail address, which turned out to be a great boon. The unforeseen horror to come—the September 11, 2001, attack on the World Trade Center and the Pentagon—had the effect of halting and then reducing travel worldwide, so that by November 2001, there were no commercial flights to Midway. From then on, only scientists and army and U.S. Fish and Wildlife personnel would go to Midway.

Using the e-mail address Flint gave me, in the fall of 2001 I wrote Professor Hasegawa, not without great trepidation. Why would a biologist, and a world-renowned one, bother with a relatively unknown U.S. writer-academic who didn't even know Japanese? Yet the reply to my query was immediate. Hiroshi Hasegawa invited me to come to Japan and accompany him on a field trip to Torishima in December 2001 to see the albatross. He also referred me to a chapter in Dianne Ackerman's *Rarest of the Rare*, in which she recounts her trip to Torishima, also at Hasegawa's invitation. Ackerman's essay describes the climb up volcanic slopes from the encampment on one side of the island to the nesting grounds of the short-tailed albatross and includes her account of swinging by rope into volcanic rock and breaking two ribs, being taken by emergency ship to Tokyo, and enduring pain for the next two years. Far less brave than she, I wrote Professor Hasegawa that I was a fifty-three-year-old woman with two daughters, and that much as I wanted to see the albatross, I didn't have the stamina required to accompany him on his fieldwork, nor was I able to take off for three weeks during a teaching semester. He kindly offered me another alternative, a cruise on a Japanese ocean liner that takes three days and circles Torishima with the express purpose of giving the passengers a look at the birds, but only from onboard ship. Another fortuitous coincidence was that the cruise schedule fell precisely within my spring break at the university, so I jumped at the chance to take the trip.

What I did not initially know about Hiroshi Hasegawa was that he was a devotee of the Manjiro story. He possesses probably the largest collection of Manjiro books: juvenile fiction, comic-book renditions, adult novels, biographies, and academic treatments. He told me that he felt serendipity guiding his footsteps as well; every time he visits a used book or an antiquarian shop, some book or other will draw him to it, and he will find himself the owner of yet another version of Manjiro's life and times. During my trip to Japan, I thus had the good fortune to peruse the Hasegawa collection, which he lugged from his office to the faculty lounge of the biology department at Toho University;

I was absorbed in the books when I found a much-needed cup of tea by my elbow. The biology graduate students noticed me and courteously made me tea without in the least obtruding on my studies.

But to begin with the beginning of the journey: In an e-mail preparatory to my visit, Hiroshi asked me what I thought I needed to see and do in Japan. I told him that it would be immensely useful for me to see Manjiro's birthplace, the village of Nakanohama at the southwestern-most point of Shikoku; to visit a museum with artifacts from the nineteenth century, both before and after the Meiji Restoration; and to speak with Manjiro's great-grandson. Of course, I said, I was aware that in the eight days I had in Japan, a visit to Shikoku was impossible (it takes at least eighteen hours by train from Tokyo to the eastern shore of Shikoku), and interviewing Dr. Nakahama, Manjiro's descendant, would be equally unlikely since I didn't speak Japanese and had no introduction to the family. But within a week, Hiroshi e-mailed me an itinerary that included not only a visit to the Sapporo Historical Museum but also a three-day trip to Shikoku, specifically to Tosashimizu (the amalgamated villages including Nakanohama), and a day trip to Nagoya to interview Dr. Nakahama. Among all these activities were the three days onboard the ocean liner that would take us around Torishima to see the albatross. That Hiroshi would arrange for me to take the cruise to Torishima on which he himself served as guide for the avid birders who form the volunteer group for the preservation of the short-tailed albatross was not perhaps so surprising, although I felt it to be a piece of great goodwill on his part, making arrangements for me and securing passage. But Hiroshi acted as my guide in every aspect of my voyage, taking charge of me from the moment I came out of the airport gates: he reserved a hotel in Chiba for me, introduced me to his friends, took me to the museum and to his office to look at his Manjiro book collection, guided me to Yokohama and the cruise ship, attended to me during the cruise, and flew with me to Kochi, the capital of the southwestern prefecture of Shikoku, where he put me in the care of a former graduate student of his, Tamayo Masui (now Izumi). Together with Tamayo and her fiancé, Jun, I went from Kochi to Tosashimizu, where Hiroshi had arranged for a translator for me, as we were to be guided by the Manjiro Society president, Mr. Myazaki, who spoke no English. Mr. Myazaki took us on a tour of the Manjiro museum, the village, and Ashizuri Cape, where he had us walk along the path of the pilgrims who worship at the twenty-eight temples along the shores of Shikoku. Because of Hiroshi's influence and that of his former student, who works in the public relations office of the prefecture, I met a number of people, journalists and writers, who all helped me with research into the story of Manjiro. In Tosashimizu, Mr.

Myazaki took me to the cemetery where Manjiro's mother had placed a very modest stone on his premature grave; since he had been gone for ten years, she was sure he had died at sea. Another acquaintance, Junya Nagakuni, himself an author of distinguished texts about Manjiro, ushered me into a Buddhist temple and showed me the records of Manjiro and his companions' arrival upon their repatriation, as well as the recording of their presumed deaths that preceded the documented return. My young guides, Tamayo and Jun, together with my translator, Arthur Davis, took me to see the huge statue of Manjiro in a public park at Ashizuri Cape.

Finally, after my return to Tokyo, Hiroshi escorted me to Nagoya to see Dr. Nakahama, the great-grandson of my protagonist, himself a well-traveled man. For the better part of an afternoon, Dr. Nakahama, who is an elderly man and was recovering from an operation, graciously showed me documents and responded to my questions.[3] That was my last full day in Japan. The next day, Hiroshi came to the hotel to take me to the airport and part from me, Japanese-style for this last time, telling me "Sayonara" and taking a short bow. We have continued our e-mail exchange, and I expect that we will remain faithful friends and correspondents for the rest of our lives. Each spring, Hiroshi lets me know of the increase in the birds' population. In the summer of 2002, he wrote me about the volcanic eruption on Torishima, which fortunately occurred while the birds were at sea. In the fall of 2004, he let me know that representatives of several governments of countries around the Pacific rim, including the United States, met in Tokyo and actually took steps to work out a plan of relocating the short-tailed albatross not only to the less dangerous slopes of Torishima but to other nesting sites on other islands, such as the Senkaku and the Ogasawara Gunto archipelagos. Aided until now solely by an artist friend who made decoys of the birds in mating poses, Hiroshi has long worked toward such relocations, which would provide greater safety for the imperiled species. My novel about Manjiro is dedicated to him, the man who has spent his career righting the balance of the world so often tilted by human greed and ignorance.

If the short-tailed albatross makes it through the perils of its minute genetic pool, the threatened eruptions on Torishima that might bury the nesting grounds in ash, and our present craving for deep-sea fish that result in long-line fishing ships trapping endangered animals and drowning them, then perhaps we should rename the Steller's species. I await a dream in which a traveler from the future shows me an ashen cliff peaked with snow—multitudes of Hasegawa's albatross, rising and falling like the squalls I know so well from winters in the American Midwest.

Notes

1. Although Manjiro brought the knowledge of the Western world's appetite for feathers to Japan, he himself did not promote the industrial-scale exploitation and killing of albatross, moving instead into the academic realm.

2. The details of Manjiro's encounter with Tamaoiki and of the near-demise of the species, as well as of their recovery, come from personal communications with Hiroshi Hasegawa.

3. Dr. Hiroshi Nakahama has kept up the tradition of the Nakahama family, according to which every eldest son of each generation succeeding Manjiro writes at least one biography of the famous predecessor.

Works Cited

Ackerman, Dianne. "Short-Tailed Albatrosses." *The Rarest of the Rare: Vanishing Animals, Timeless Worlds*. New York: Random, 1995. 43–93.

Steiner, Rick. "Resurrection in the Wind." *National Wildlife Magazine*, Aug.-Sept. 1998: 1–8.

Vlasopolos, Anca. *The New Bedford Samurai*. Kingsport, TN: Twilight Times, 2007.

17

Stumbling in the Archives
A Tale of Two Novices

Lisa Mastrangelo and Barbara L'Eplattenier

Recently, we were honored to be on-line guest lecturers in a rhetoric and composition graduate methodology class. The teacher of the class wrote to us that he couldn't find anything about "doing" archival work—could we please fill in the blanks? This unnerved us a bit as neither of us had had any specific training in archival work. We just wandered in one day, sat down at the table, and started thumbing through boxes and boxes of old dusty, tattered papers. We had none of what John Brereton says historians need—the "combination of paleography and the appropriate languages and . . . working knowledge of the relevant online and print bibliographies" (575) that makes archival work so much easier. We knew little of the archives available to us and had little understanding of how archives function or how to work effectively with archivists. We didn't know about indices and standard texts. We didn't know about grants. We didn't have texts such as this to refer to. We were fools rushing in where angels fear to tread.

But we were happy.

We took into the archives a fascination with the lives of the women we had been researching, an insatiable curiosity about them, a willingness to do detective work, and a determination to find answers to our questions about them. As Robert Connors notes in "Dreams and Play," "the Archive is where storage meets dreams, and the result is history" (17). We took with us the blessings and support of our teachers and their belief in our ability to do this work.

We've learned a lot since we first began—enough so that in 2004 we co-edited *Historical Studies of Writing Program Administration: Individuals, Communities, and the Formation of a Discipline.* Most of the essays in *Historical Studies* draw on archival research in order to present the first sustained examination of the historical roots of writing program administration. The experience and our many discussions with the authors about their archival work enriched our own knowledge immeasurably. So it's a pleasure to talk about our archival experiences, our love for the people we study, and the work we do.

Barb

I have been sitting in the Vassar College archives. Modeled after a European castle, the library has huge stained glass windows, buttressed arches, and glorious high ceilings. It looks and feels more like a church than a library. The archives have recently been renovated. They are sleek and modern with tubal furniture, located deep in the library's basement.

All day, I revel in the lives of women who lived a hundred years ago. I peer at their portraits, read their personal letters detailing travels down the Hudson to New York City to march in the suffrage parade, thumb through memos about light bulbs and pleas for mimeograph machines. I am transported.

At closing time, I stumble up the stairs and out the front door. I blink dumbly in the bright summer sunshine, certain I see young women dressed in long skirts and mutton-sleeve blouses laughing and talking under the huge oak tree on the Vassar lawn. It takes a long time to return to the twentieth century.

Neither one of us went to graduate school thinking we were going to be rhetoric and composition historians, much less archival historians. Like our first trips into the archives, we discovered our research areas serendipitously. Barb compared the history she was studying in one class with the current status of composition and asked, "When and how did this change?," while Lisa wanted to know about the history of writing instruction at nineteenth-century women's colleges. This curiosity led Barb to Vassar, where she studied how Laura Wylie and Gertrude Buck ran the turn-of-the-century English department, and Lisa to Mount Holyoke and Wellesley, where she studied Clara Stevens and Sophie Chantal Hart. After years of reading their papers and secondary sources about them, we know these women as well as, if not better than, our own families. Such passion and questioning are the historian's most valued characteristics. Rejecting blanket assumptions about how people did things or about current traditions is how historians are born.

Lisa

I am in the cafeteria of the state university where I am completing my graduate work, desperately reading James Berlin's Rhetoric and Reality *before I meet with my mentor. It is one of the only books about the history of rhetoric and composition available to me and is a near-biblical text in rhetoric and composition. I read a passage that tells me that Mount Holyoke College, my alma mater, had an undergraduate degree in rhetoric*

*at the turn of the century (56)—the turn of the nineteenth century. I am
thrilled. I've heard of English degrees, but never a degree in rhetoric given
at the undergraduate level. I am perplexed. The graduate student I am
sitting with does not share my wonder. She asks me who cares. I do.*

*My curiosity leads me to the Mount Holyoke archives in South Hadley,
Massachusetts. Why would they have a degree in rhetoric when no one else
had such a thing? The archivist shows me the English department records,
dating back to the college's founding in 1837, and I begin to poke and sift.
I make some notes. I mark some items for photocopying. I don't know
what I'm doing, and I really don't know how to find what I'm looking
for. The archivist goes to lunch, and the assistant archivist inquires about
my project. As we chat, she asks if I have seen Clara Stevens's papers. I
have never heard of her. Clara received one of the first master's degrees in
rhetoric awarded from the University of Michigan. Consequently, she ran
the Mount Holyoke department and the undergraduate major in rhetoric
for thirty-seven years. Clara Stevens is why there was a degree in rhetoric
at Mount Holyoke. Clara Stevens becomes the topic of my dissertation.*

As we talk with scholars, we find that our stories—stumbling into archives,
fascinated but untrained in historiographical methods—are not unique. Most
of us in the humanities were, after all, trained in literary analysis, where the
text (usually) appears complete before you. We didn't know how to construct
historical narratives or read census data or hunt down archival documents.
Even famed rhetoric and composition historian Robert Connors, with years
of archival research behind him, offered the seemingly simplistic advice to
approach archival research as a directed ramble, an August mushroom hunt
(23). Interesting, but unhelpful when faced with an unfamiliar finding aid.

Barb

*I visit an archive to research a woman who ran a large English department
at a normal school. The archives are located in the basement, with pipes
and exposed wiring running along the ceiling. Piles and piles of things fill
up the room; there's almost no space to work; and there is a devoted and
fierce archivist with minimal resources. No catalogue, no index, no list. I
keep asking for "stuff on the English department," and the archivist looks
at me thoughtfully, nodding her head and saying, "We don't have that, but
this might interest you." The unreliable wiring in the basement won't support a photocopy machine, so all documents have to be copied on the second
floor common access photocopy machine. Kids are photocopying lecture*

*notes from biology class. I'm feeding in dimes and copying 120-year-old
documents that are ready to fall apart. It's all a little disconcerting.*

As we look over archival materials, we know we make educated guesses.
We do not work with complete pictures, nor can we ever truly create them.
We know that human beings have left these records and sorted through them,
and as a result, they are flawed. We know that our research only scratches the
surface of what a time period or event was like. We try not to cling too tightly
to a hypothesis—or to wander around the archives without one. Doing either
one puts us in a position of danger. We might ignore—or not see—what the
archives tell us. Like the biologist Barbara McClintock, we work to hear the
stories of the archives and adapt accordingly (qtd. in Belenky 143–44). Like
any good storyteller, we have to be patient and listen, figuring out where our
piece fits. Listening lets us understand a document that has previously made
no sense. Listening lets us place it into a constantly shifting paradigm.

Lisa

*I am sitting with the assistant archivist at Mount Holyoke College, look-
ing at an alumnae survey filled out and signed by Clara Stevens. We
cannot make sense of it. The survey is dated after Clara's death. We spend
the afternoon thinking. Finally, the archivist pulls out the survey filled out
by Clara's sister, Alice. For some reason, rather than reporting her death,
Alice has filled out her sister's survey and signed it. Her spidery handwriting is so similar to Clara's that we didn't notice.*

We have worked to develop a sense of what to do with archival documents
once we have them. We puzzle over what it means to accurately (and we hesi-
tate to use that word) present the men and women whose documents we are
exploring. We struggle to keep in mind our subjectivity, our positions, our
ideological lenses, our own agendas. It takes us a long time to understand
archival documents because there is nothing to read them against, nothing to
hold them up to in order to compare.

It seems to be human nature to create a smooth, cohesive whole instead of
settling for disparate parts. We like to work with texts that are complete, and
archival work instead requires us to work with fragments. We long for a plot,
a hero, a villain, a conflict, a resolution. But we would do well to remember
that there are no smooth, unified stories. The stories are rough and bumpy
with false starts and misleading paths, populated with non-heroic, fragile,
determined, tenacious people who went about their daily business, focused
on their own goals and their own desires. Attempts to overanalyze—to litera-

cize—do them a disservice. We should remember that, ultimately, historians are storytellers.

Lisa

I am at the Wellesley archives, looking at the papers of Sophie Chantal Hart. Hart chaired the Wellesley English department for thirty-eight years. She was beloved by her students, and I read one memorial tribute after another praising her wonderful teaching. However, Patricia Palmieri, in her book In Adamless Eden, *describes Hart as "aggressive," "verbally adept," and "one of several warring giants" on campus (129). A colleague accuses her of trying "to get people to work for her as much as possible" (128). As much as I want to, I cannot ignore the criticism and only focus on the praise. It is tempting to erase this aspect of her personality, but it is a part of who Hart was, and while it complicates her history, it also makes it richer. I cannot ignore the disparity that I see in these documents.*

Connections between researchers can be marred by competitiveness, and yet these connections are vital for sharing work, ideas, and even documents. Our own experiences clearly demonstrate this. We first met at a break-out session of a meeting of the Coalition of Women Scholars in the History of Rhetoric and Composition, where we discovered we were working on similar areas of research. Both doctoral students at the time, we each felt like we'd found a long-lost soul mate. Our connection to one another has been a lifeline.

The Progressive Era that we study—that dynamic and turbulent time period between approximately 1890 and 1920—seems to get short shrift within rhetoric and composition histories. Few texts contextualize events within the era itself. It is often the *end* of the story, rather than the beginning. For us, the Progressive Era and its upheaval—the founding of colleges, the beginning of departmentalization, the rise in women's education, and the rise in an interest in teaching writing—is *the* story.

As a result, we rely extensively on each other. We share stories and resources. We argue about what things "mean." We review each other's drafts. We pass on information about new books—usually out of women's studies or educational studies. (Lynn D. Gordon's *Gender and Higher Education in the Progressive Era* and Barbara Miller Solomon's *In the Company of Educated Women* have been particularly useful.)

The community we found in the archives and in each other, we also found as we worked on *Historical Studies of Writing Program Administration*. When the book made its appearance at the 2004 Conference on College Composition and Communication, we asked the contributors to join us at a celebratory dinner.

The result was an evening of laughter and conversation, with people trading stories about their archival experiences. Our research has opened up our circle of friends, both living and dead. We know well those who administered writing programs before us: June Rose Colby, Edwin Hopkins, George Wykoff, and Gertrude Buck. We know those who write about them: Randy Popkins, Shirley Rose, Deany Cheramie, Amy Heckathorn, Lynee Gaillet. Just as we need access to documents and to archives, we need access to one another.

Most important, we've encouraged each other's projects and developed new ones, both separately and together. The work we do is less "mine" and "yours" than "ours." Our work would not take the shape it does without each other's input.

> *Barb*
>
> *In one of our many early morning phone calls to each other, Lisa mentions she found this funny thing—this sort of transcript—in the Wellesley archives from a gathering at Mount Holyoke. The names listed are names we know—old friends from our doctoral work: Clara, Laura, Sophie, Gertrude, Mary Yost, Mary Augusta Jordon, Ada Snell.*
>
> *"It's really weird," she says. "There's like twenty women there, in 1919, all talking about writing at their own colleges. It's almost like a Q and A—whoever transcribed it took down what each speaker was saying. And Clara has written little corrections in the margins and initialed them."*
>
> *"Huh—1919. I think I have a memo from Gertrude Buck to President McCracken asking for permission to have a meeting like that at Vassar. That was '22 or '23—she had the stroke, so it never happened. Hang on, let me check."*

Out of that conversation came our co-authored "'Is It the Pleasure of this Conference to Have Another?' Women's Colleges Meeting and Talking about Writing in the Progressive Era." Although we knew our women talked and thought about writing at their own schools, that transcript helped us realize that there was a community, an early version of the contemporary writing program administrators community, among the forerunners of the Seven Sisters colleges. This community worried about admissions testing, training, standards, curriculum—all the things the rhetoric and composition community worries about today. Without our early morning and late night conversations with each other and with other researchers, such work might never come to fruition.

We understand that the past pulls us forward—all of us endlessly recycle and reuse that which has come before us, all the while claiming it to be new and unique. More and more, we recognize that intertextuality refers not only to the written word but to everything. To know the past is to comprehend the future.

Barb and Lisa

While vacationing together in Switzerland in the summer of 2004, we decide to visit the Abbey Library of St. Gallen, a 223-year-old scriptorium with books from the ninth century.[1] Barb's Swiss-born aunt repeatedly tells us not to go to St. Gallen. "It's a dump!" she says vehemently. Others clearly look puzzled when we tell them of our plans.

The wooden library floors are original—beautiful inlaid fleur-de-lis made with four or five different types of wood. They are kept clean and polished because all visitors must wear oversized felt slippers. We skate awkwardly, hands clasped behind our backs, along the exhibition cases.

The shelves extend up two levels, from the floor to the ceiling. The docent shows us that each column in between the shelves opens and contains a type of movable card catalogue so that users can easily locate texts. The cards are marked with the title, the author, where the book came from, and when the library acquired it; the cards themselves date back hundreds of years. The library is both an architect's and a researcher's dream.

The exhibit is called A Thousand Years of Charlemagne's Influence, and some of the manuscripts shown are from Charlemagne's teacher, Alcuin—who, we discover, wrote a rhetoric. An early copy of one of Boethius's works is also on display. We are enthralled—by the floor-to-ceiling books, the card catalogue, the polished wood, the baroque ceilings and trim, the possibility of research.

It is researcher's serendipity—finding artifacts that cause us to ask questions. We even know where we can find the answers, if only we spoke the language! On the train ride back to our hotel, we plot sabbaticals in Switzerland, brainstorm grant possibilities, theorize about research questions, create lists of sources, and try to figure out how quickly we can learn Old German. Far too soon, we arrive back at our destination.

The St. Gallen scriptorium demonstrated to us how far we have come. As researchers, we have built a heuristic base upon which to work. We know enough to think about letters of introduction, to sign up for grant alerts, to search the databases for additional archival documents, to generate heuristics about our subjects. While the joy of discovery and serendipity remains the same, we are no longer stumbling in the archives. Instead, we have become seasoned explorers who know enough to outfit ourselves with pencils (pens make marks on the documents), lots of change (for photocopying), a structured method of pulling boxes (so you don't look at the same ones twice), and a box of donuts or bottle of wine for the archivist.

We have large questions to ask about doing archival work and only small answers to share. We share our stories and our experiences, hoping they draw attention to the need for greater interest in and training for archival research, but also with the hope that our enthusiasm, our love of the August mushroom hunt, will be passed on to someone else.

Note

1. For the scriptorium, see *Stiftsbibliothek St. Gallen* at <http://www.stibi. ch/index.asp>.

Works Cited

Belenky, Mary, et al. *Women's Way's of Knowing: The Development of Self, Voice, and Mind.* New York: HarperCollins, 1986.

Berlin, James. *Rhetoric and Reality: Writing Instruction in American Colleges, 1900–1985.* Carbondale: Southern Illinois UP, 1987.

Brereton, John. "Rethinking Our Archive: A Beginning." *College English* 61 (1999): 574–76.

Connors, Robert. "Dreams and Play: Historical Method and Methodology." *Methods and Methodology in Composition Research.* Ed. Gesa E. Kirsch and Patricia Sullivan. Carbondale: Southern Illinois UP, 1992. 15–36.

Ferreira-Buckley, Linda. "Rescuing the Archives from Foucault." *College English* 61 (1999): 577–83.

Gordon, Lynn D. *Gender and Higher Education in the Progressive Era.* New Haven: Yale UP, 1990.

L'Eplattenier, Barbara, and Lisa Mastrangelo, eds. *Historical Studies of Writing Program Administration: Individuals, Communities, and the Formation of a Discipline.* West Lafayette, IN: Parlor, 2004.

Mastrangelo, Lisa, and Barbara L'Eplattenier. "'Is It the Pleasure of this Conference to Have Another?' Women's Colleges Meeting and Talking about Writing in the Progressive Era." L'Eplattenier and Mastrangelo 117–44.

Mattingly, Carol. *Well-Tempered Women: Nineteenth-Century Temperance Rhetoric.* Carbondale: Southern Illinois UP, 1998.

Miller, Thomas, and Melody Bowdon. "A Rhetorical Stance on the Archives of Civic Action." *College English* 61 (1999): 591–98.

Palmieri, Patricia. *In Adamless Eden: The Community of Women Faculty at Wellesley.* New Haven: Yale UP, 1995.

Pfaelzer, Jean. *Parlor Radical: Rebecca Harding Davis and the Origins of American Social Realism.* Pittsburgh: U of Pittsburgh P, 1997.

Royster, Jacqueline Jones. *Traces of a Stream: Literacy and Social Change among African American Women.* Pittsburgh: U of Pittsburgh P, 2000.

Solomon, Barbara Miller. *In the Company of Educated Women: A History of Women in Higher Education in America.* New Haven: Yale UP, 1985.

Contributors

ELIZABETH (BETSY) BIRMINGHAM teaches professional writing and gender studies in the English department at North Dakota State University. Her research concerns the role of women in architectural practice and history; she has published this scholarship in architecture, rhetoric, and women's studies journals.

KATE DAVY is a professor of English and the dean of arts and sciences at Bentley College. Her research interests include feminist critical theory and avant-garde performance. Her most recent scholarly book, *Lady Dicks and Lesbian Brothers: Making Theater in the WOW Café*, is forthcoming.

W. RALPH EUBANKS, a writer and editor based in Washington, D.C., is the author of *Ever Is a Long Time: A Journey into Mississippi's Dark Past*, which *Washington Post* book critic Jonathan Yardley named as one of the best non-fiction books of 2003. Eubanks has contributed articles to the *Washington Post* Outlook, Style, Health, and BookWorld sections; the *Chicago Tribune*; *Preservation*; and National Public Radio. Since 1995, he has been the director of publishing at the Library of Congress.

DAVID GOLD is an assistant professor of English at California State University, Los Angeles, where he teaches courses in rhetoric, writing, and English pedagogy. His scholarship has been published in *College English, College Composition and Communication, Rhetoric Review*, and other journals. His recently completed book is *Rhetoric at the Margins: Revising the History of Writing Instruction in American Colleges, 1873–1947* (2008).

GESA E. KIRSCH teaches in the English department at Bentley College. Her research interests include feminism and composition, ethics, qualitative research methods, and women's autobiography. She has written and edited numerous books, mostly recently *Feminism and Composition: A Critical Sourcebook* (2003).

BARBARA L'EPLATTENIER works in the Rhetoric and Writing Department at the University of Arkansas–Little Rock. With Lisa Mastrangelo, she co-edited *Historical Studies of Writing Program Administration: Individuals, Communities, and the Formation of a Discipline* (2004), which won the WPA Best Book of the Year Award in 2005.

LISA MASTRANGELO teaches writing and literature and is the coordinator of women's studies at the College of St. Elizabeth. With Barbara L'Eplattenier, she has recently published the collection *Historical Studies of Writing Program Administration*.

ALICIA NITECKI teaches in the English department at Bentley College. Her research interests include creative writing (the personal essay), medieval literature, and the Holocaust. Nitecki is the author of *Recovered Land* (1995), *Jakub's World* (2005), and six translations of Polish works on the Holocaust, including Janusz Nel Siedlecki, Krystyn Olszewski, and Tadeusz Borowski's *We Were in Auschwitz* (2000).

GAIL Y. OKAWA is a professor of English at Youngstown State University (Ohio), where she teaches courses in American multicultural studies, life-writing studies, and sociolinguistics. She is the author of numerous articles on the politics of language, literacy, culture, and identity and is currently completing a book-length study on the little-known captivity and literacy experiences of Hawai'i's Japanese immigrants who were subjected to U.S. Justice Department internment during World War II.

MALEA POWELL is the director of rhetoric and writing at Michigan State University and is the editor of the journal *SAIL: Studies in American Indian Literature*. Her edited volume *Of Color: Native American Literatures* is forthcoming.

BARRY ROHAN has been a reporter at large midwestern metropolitan newspapers, including the *Milwaukee Sentinel*, the *Minneapolis Tribune*, and the *Detroit Free Press*, for thirty years. He is currently a freelance writer in the Detroit area.

LIZ ROHAN teaches in the English department at the University of Michigan–Dearborn. Her research interests include feminist research methodologies, computers and writing, writing centers, literacy studies, creative nonfiction/life writing, and American studies. She has published several articles about women and literacy; her latest appeared in the winter 2006 issue of *Pedagogy*.

LUCILLE M. SCHULTZ is a professor of English at the University of Cincinnati. Her most recent book, *Archives of Instruction* (with J. Ferguson Carr and S. Carr, 2005), won the 2006 Mina P. Shaughnessy Prize from the Modern Language Association, and her 1999 *The Young Composers* won the Nancy Dasher Prize from the College English Association of Ohio in 2000. Her research interests include the history of composition instruction in nineteenth-century schools and colleges; girls' literacies in the nineteenth century; the authorship, publication, and reception histories of nineteenth-century composition texts; and composition theory and pedagogy.

WENDY B. SHARER teaches in the English department at East Carolina University. Sharer published *Vote and Voice: Women's Organizations and Political Literacy, 1915–1930* (2004) and also co-edited the anthology *Rhetorical Education in America* (2004).

RONALD R. STOCKTON is a professor of political science at the University of Michigan–Dearborn. He is the author of *Decent and in Order: Conflict, Christianity and Polity in a Presbyterian Congregation* (2000) and is co-author, with Frank Wayman, of *A Time of Turmoil: Values and Voting in the 1970s* (1982). He has written numerous academic articles.

CHRISTINE MASON SUTHERLAND is a scholar and teacher of the history of rhetoric at the University of Calgary. She has published numerous peer-reviewed articles and is the co-author of two edited collections. Her most recent book, *The Eloquence of Mary Astell*, was published in 2005.

VICTOR VILLANUEVA is the Edward R. Meyer Distinguished Professor of Liberal Arts at Washington State University. Villanueva has published both scholarly and creative works, including the award-winning memoir *Bootstraps: From an American Academic of Color* (1993).

ANCA VLASOPOLOS teaches English and comparative literature at Wayne State University. She publishes both scholarly and creative works, most recently *Penguins in a Warming World* (2007) and *The New Bedford Samurai* (2007) as well as *No Return Address: A Memoir of Displacement* (2000).

KATHLEEN WIDER is a professor of philosophy at the University of Michigan–Dearborn. Wider is the author of *The Bodily Nature of Consciousness: Sartre and Contemporary Philosophy of Mind* (1997) and is at work on a book tentatively titled *A Woman in a Treeless Landscape*, in which she reflects on issues of selfhood in the context of her grandmother's life.